Two Centuries, One Year

A Historical Novel of the First World War

Ann Calwell

Hart + Harvest Press

Cover by Kostis Pavlou.

First Hart + Harvest Edition published 2025.

hartandharvest.com

***

To all my students

***

Preface

This is a work of fiction, but it is based on true events. It takes place in the town where I grew up: Nitro, West Virginia, still known today as an engineering marvel. It is a story of the remarkable change thrust upon the town in the early twentieth Century as it moved, over the course of mere months, from farmland to an industrial hub providing significant support to the United States' efforts in World War I.

On October 6, 1917, Congress passed the Deficiency Appropriations Act for the construction of three plants capable of producing five hundred thousand pounds of gunpowder per day for use in fighting Germany in World War I. The village that would become Nitro was selected by War Department engineers as an ideal location, as it was protected from coastal attacks while having easy access to rail and river transportation. On December 23, 1917, ground was broken to build Explosives Plant C in only ten months. Change was rapid, and war profiteering—though never proven—was suspected to run rampant.

Decades later, a resolution was entered into the *Congressional Record* during the proceedings of the 97th Congress, Second Session. West Virginia Senator Robert C. Byrd asked "that the United States Senate designate the city of Nitro, West Virginia, as a living memorial to our victorious role in The Great War against Germany, and to those who fought the war or worked to win it." My father, Jack Moody, and

William Wentz, both living in Nitro, worked with Senator John D. Rockefeller IV to urge Congress to adopt the resolution. On December 29, 1982, Senate Resolution 487 officially recognized the city of Nitro as a living memorial to World War I.

Nitro spent 1918 hurtling from one century into the next. In this work, I have reimagined this transformation through the eyes of a twelve-year-old girl, Ana Ariano—a young "war correspondent" with a fertile mind and a front-row seat to the changes occurring around her.

I have included in this story a collection of historical photographs from World War I, including many from the archive of Explosives Plant C. While the photographs are real, any reference to characters in the captions are imagined, and included to help immerse the reader in Ana's tale.

Ann Calwell
September 2025

Contents

The Pupils Must Learn!

I write this down in sadness. Everyone in the whole world is in grave danger.

My name is Ana Ariano. I am twelve years old. Everything I know and everything I believe in has exploded. War has exploded.

Mother says that these times are very important, and I should write everything down so that I will remember it forever. She means it, but I am also pretty sure she will read everything I write. There is a lot to write down, so here goes.

Pearl Ariano

This Great War started nearly four years ago, and since then every-thing I know about the world is falling apart and collapsing into war.

President Wilson understood that the United States of America could not escape the flames of war. The world cannot keep on burning—so last year he joined with the other countries fighting the Germans. More than twenty countries are on our side!

Tanks such as this one were used in trench warfare.

This war is different from anything anybody has ever seen before. The Germans have submarines under the water that keep sinking ships, and airplanes come out of the sky. The British invented a new weapon called the tank. The picture I saw is a terrible thing, like a big fast turtle that shoots at soldiers from the huge gun on the top—or can just roll over German soldiers where they are standing.

The Germans have made machine guns that can fire six hundred bullets in one minute. New cannons can kill thousands of men with their powerful shells. Hand grenades can explode in a small space. Other weapons can blow trees right out of the ground.

Horse wearing gas mask

There are also new gas weapons: sulfur dioxide, mustard gas that leaves blisters, and tear gas that can blind the soldiers. Even the brave horses must wear gas masks—ugly sacks strapped like a feed bag over their noses and mouths. But even these masks will not work against something called phosgene gas. In France, even children are practicing how to wear gas masks.

On the most horrible days, fifty thousand people die. It is too terribly sad.

A lot is needed for us to win the war. We need weapons like guns, gunpowder, and shells, and we will need to send our soldiers food and clothes too.

Every day in school, we learn from our book *School History of the Great War*. We learned that Germany, even if it already has a lot of power, wants even more.

The Germans say they deserve a place in the sun. I copied this out. They want to push other countries out of the way so they can have everything they want. I am sure they want the United States of America. They would stop mail and school and everything else that is important here.

Ammunition

They are our Great Enemies in this Total War. That is what we learn in school. Tomorrow at school we will talk about if it is fair for one country to rule another country just because they believe that their own ideas are better than everybody else's. Missus Marsh is talking about Germany, and the answer is NO!

Tonight, I must learn all the reasons why Germany really wanted this war. I will study very hard for this test.

1. War means profit for the winners. The President said a strong NO to this and an even stronger NO to war profiteering! It is hard to believe this really happens—that there are people out there who would really try to profit from a war.

2. Winning the war would mean Germany gets more land from other countries.

3. The German army wants to humiliate France, and if Germany wins, they will take the iron mines in France.

4. Belgium has a lot of coal. Germany needs more coal, so they want to use the war to make Belgium part of their country.

5. Germany wants Holland for a path to the sea.

6. Germany wants to win the war so they can get more food for German people.

7. If Germany wins the war, every country they gobble up will have to pay money to Germany. This is called indemnity. But if we win the war and they lose, Germany will have to pay lots of money for all the damage from the war. This makes sense to me because they started the war in the first place.

8. Germany wants to Germanize the world. They believe they need more—more land and more resources and more people. They believe only the fittest people should survive!

Children holding "NO COAL" sign

The battles in the trenches are horrible beyond belief. The trenches are six feet deep and very long, like mole tunnels or the trail of a giant snail. The armies use barbed wire and booby traps and sandbags to protect them. Every time there is an explosion, they must build the trench over again. When it rains the trenches flood, and they have to pump all the water out. It makes mud that can be fifteen feet deep. The smell must be awful.

Think of the trenches as sausage machines. So many of our brave soldiers are killed—Missus Marsh told us that.

Death is all around. There are even suicide pacts when the trenches are impossible to endure. Everything we learn makes me so sad.

That is why I must find a way to help us win the war. I am promising this tonight. I will find a way to help the President bring victory to America.

Brave Little Belgium

I was just taking care of Mabel. She is one of our best champion horses. Strong but gentle. Big hooves. Bright eyes.

American horses will win this war for us—I just know it!

We learned in school that this war started in the year 1914 when someone got killed. The Germans marched soldiers into Belgium first and took over the people and the land. Next they wanted to march into France and take over there. They marched and marched all the way to thirty miles away from Paris. French people love their France the way we love our America, so six thousand Frenchmen rushed to help fight. They even rode in taxicabs to go fight!

Britain already said they would send soldiers to fight Germany if Germany invaded Belgium and so they did—and just like Britain went to war because of Belgium, President Wilson says that we must go to war because Germany is fighting Britain. Fighting Britain is the same as if Germany went to war against America. So we must join in.

The President says huge sacrifices will be necessary. There will be lots of death and not a whole lot of food to go around. We are going to have to send thousands and thousands of soldiers to France—maybe even one million! Americans fighting in Europe for Britain and France. I do not know if this ever happened before.

War is everywhere now. It is on the land and in the skies and under the ocean—with new scary weapons. The new weapons mean death and more death. So many brave soldiers are dying.

Missus Marsh is very nice. She knows how war scares us all. We learn all sorts of things about the war in school, and other things too.

I have been trying to learn even more about the war outside of school because it is all so scary. I read that the Germans started planning this war nine years before it even started. When the French soldiers rushed in to fight, they had to charge right into German machine guns that could shoot very fast. The French fighters only had rifles and bayonets. There were more than one million casualties.

Every new weapon has a new answer, like scopes that British soldiers can use to shoot from very far away. The Germans build trenches too—trenches that are many miles long. They cannot be seen on the other side because they go down into the ground and they have barbed wire. The Germans made flame-throwers that can hold one thousand pounds of explosives. It terrifies enemy soldiers who fear they will be burned to death. Soon, France got their own flame-throwers. And Britain invented the tank—a strong weapon that can blast right through the trenches.

I read that Germany has twelve thousand guns and more than two million shells for their cannons. They might be burned up. I guess we will need a lot more guns—and a lot more bullets—and a lot more GUNPOWDER.

Mother told my sister Sarah and me to read about Belgium in her magazine.

Tell everyone you talk to about it—Mother said this. And she is right. The world must know. I tore a story out of her magazine so I can show it to everybody at school. The magazine is named *The Delineator*, and the story is called "Brave Little Belgium."

In Brave Little Belgium only German newspapers are allowed. Anybody selling any other newspapers gets shot. They shoot people on bicycles, people who have pigeons that could send out letters, and anybody else who could be sending a message outside of Belgium. People are not allowed to make pictures. But the Belgian children are very brave—they make fun of the way the German soldiers march. This makes the soldiers very angry.

The German soldiers' belt buckles say "Gott mit uns," which means God is with us. I cannot believe God would want what is happening to Brave Little Belgium—Sarah agrees.

Brave Little Belgium has a saying also: Always oppressed, never defeated.

After I read Mother's magazine, I got so worried about Belgium that I forgot to do my evening chores.

More Horror

When Sarah and my fast friend Ann and I went around spreading the news about Brave Little Belgium, we told old Missus Beckley, who must be about one hundred years old. She is always sweeping in front of her house with a broom. Mister Beckley is an old cuss too.

She said she knows so much more than little girls could ever know. I think she believes she is the only person who knows anything! She might even think she knows more than President Wilson.

Missus Beckley told us how the Germans destroyed the Grand Castle in Belgium and even burned down a cathedral. We already knew this from *The Delineator*. I am a polite person, so I pretended to be in terrible shock—Ann did not.

We knew all that already, Ann said right to Missus Beckley. I would never say this to a grownup.

Missus Beckley frowned at us and made a sound from her nose that sounded like an old pig rooting about. She snorted that us young ladies should have better manners.

Well, old ladies should not pretend they know everything—Ann said this exactly!

I did not have to pretend to be shocked then, because I really was. I could feel my face getting red. We left as fast as we could to go tell the next house about Brave Little Belgium. We told them Brave Little Belgium has a saying: always oppressed, never defeated.

I am starting a list of everyone I know in case they can help America win the war.

Helpers

- Felice Ariano is my daddy—the best oxen driver of all. He hauls heavy!

- Pearl Ariano is my mother—grows food in our garden, sews clothes, knits socks, makes quilts.

- Ana Ariano is me. Good with horses.

- John Ariano is my brother—twenty years old—he got injured but he is ready to help. He is a pinsetter at the bowling alley.

- Sarah Ariano is my sister—nine years old—her rumors are not helpful.

- Ellen Ariano is my sister—seven years old—has a pretend friend named Ruby Lips—wants to help.

- Ann Moody is my new fast friend—twelve years old—a good helper.

- Harry Moody is Ann's brother—nine years old—not very helpful.

- Abigail Palmer is my second fast friend—twelve years old—another good helper. Her new brother Owen was only just born, so he is too little to help.

- Elise and Emmaline are both twelve years old—bullies—no help at all right now. I am sure they will see how much we can help achieve victory and have a change of heart.

- Noble Carter is twelve years old. He knows all about mules.

Owen Palmer

How to Help

- Raise more chickens to sell for food and eggs.

- Sell things for war money like posters so we could give money to Belgium. I might draw a poster—girls and boys knitting socks for the soldiers.

- Buy war bonds.

- Put on a talent show for money—Ann can dance, and Abigail can sing. Elise and Emmaline can tap dance and do ballet. I truly believe they will help out.

- Sell rides on Mabel for five cents every ride.

Daddy needs me at the barn right now—that is all I can write down.

The Contract

A miracle has happened! Our village is going to be very important to help win the Great War after all!

The President of the United States of America, Mister Woodrow Wilson, is directing America to build three huge plants so that each can make a share of five hundred thousand pounds of explosive gunpowder every day to help in the fight against the Germans. And we will be making one of these plants right here in our village! It has to be finished in nine months—everyone will be awfully busy. Our President is also ordering complete reports of this project, and pictures too!

I should have known that something very big and important was happening because last month two important men came to see Daddy. They stayed over one hour to meet up and talk. That is when I met Ann and Abigail—I will write about that soon. After they left, Daddy sat down on a chair in the kitchen for a bit smoking his pipe. He stared all around the room and shook his head. I asked him who the men were—he said engineers and stopped. I knew better than to ask more questions.

Just think about it—five hundred thousand pounds of gunpowder every day must be enough to blast the Germans all the way back to Germany! Britain and France need it right now. They only have one half of the ammunition they need.

I worry every day and every night about Germany's evil plans. The call has been put out for one million American fighters—that is almost everybody in West Virginia!

On January 18th, 1918, President Wilson ordered a legal contract to be signed between the United States of America and The Thompson-Starrett Company on Wall Street in New York. The contract is written in lots of pamphlets so anybody can read it. It says that we will make all of this gunpowder in nine months. Workers will be coming here from all over to get it done.

We have to do it! We can and we will! It is a war emergency alright. We had to talk to Missus Beckley again—she says the United States government is going to pay for everything we need. The food and houses for workers—all of it. Her sneaky smile makes Ann so mad.

A gentleman named Mister D.C. Jackling is the executive leader who signed the contract. It got endorsed. Daddy says he is a businessman from out west who was appointed the director of the three new government explosive plants.

The pamphlet says that the United States will pay fifty million dollars for this war emergency—some of the other numbers in the contract are marked out because they are top secret. Daddy heard the real number is closer to seven hundred and seventy million dollars. So much money will be coming to our village.

Now I understand why Mister Moody and Mister Palmer came to see Daddy around Christmastime. They are chemical engineers, so they know all about the chemicals we need to make gunpowder—like strong acid and more. They will be the leaders of this project and already knew about it when they came to see Daddy. They need land. And they need Daddy. He is the best oxen driver around—they need him to clear trees and make the earth ready. We will need a lot of space for this plant.

It is a true war emergency! Clear trees! Make explosives!!

It is as if two centuries are happening at the same time, colliding and crashing like two great rivers when they meet. Farmers will be tilling their fields like always right next to scientists using brand-new science to make weapons. It is hard to imagine, but it is going to happen!

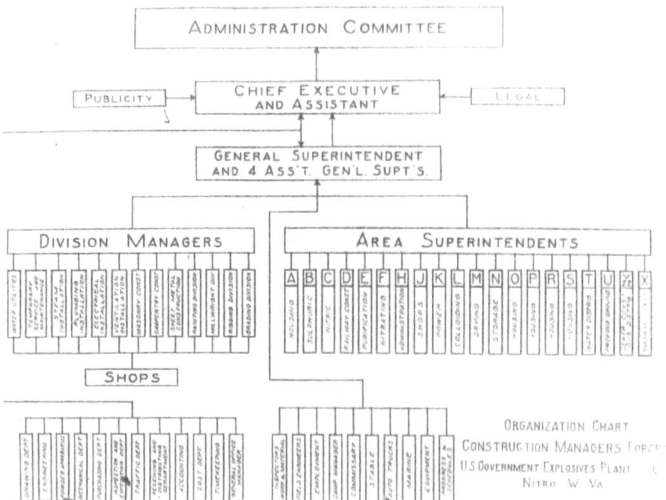

Organizational chart used in plan for Explosives Plant C

We will blow up all the German tanks. I think five hundred thousand pounds of gunpowder ought to be enough to get that done! What will happen first? What about our village?

The contract is hard to understand—maybe harder than anything I have ever read before. Even before I start my lessons I am copying out some of Article 1 of the contract to describe the plans:

1. Manage, lay out, construct, erect, and install all the buildings.

2. Manage houses, warehouses, hospitals, stores, commissaries, structures, plant, and machinery.

3. Manage railways, roads, sewerage, water and lighting systems, grading, purchasing of locomotive cars, fixtures, tools, equipment, apparatus, and appurtenances, and make sure that in eleven months the local powder plant can produce five hundred thousand pounds of powder.

This is the biggest job I have ever heard of! I heard that some very famous people are going to help—like Missus John D. Rockefeller Junior, who is going to sort out where women will live when they come to work here. I am going to keep the pamphlet about the contract with me all the time so that I can answer questions for people—they are already asking me about it, even though they could just read it for themselves. But I am always happy to help.

I bet Mother will read this so I will write this—I want to move to a new house next to the new plant so we can be as helpful as possible!

Time to water the horses, so that is all for now.

Fast Friends

I will always have dear memories about meeting Ann and Abigail. We met when Mister Moody—Ann's daddy—and Mister Palmer—Abigail's daddy—came to our village to see Daddy. Yes—the chemical engineers! I remember the exact date because it was Christmastime—the twenty-first day in December.

They said they had come with direct orders from Mister D.C. Jackling to find people who would work to clear the banks on the Great Kanawha River and haul the trees for lumber. We did not know then that the order came directly from President Wilson. We also did not know that the order was part of the plan to meet the war emergency. If they told Daddy all about it, he did not tell us right then.

My daddy, Felice Ariano, is the best oxen driver ever. Everybody knows that. He came from Ariano in Italy—Ariano, like our name. When he got married to my mother, Pearl, we got our farm and then John and Sarah and Ellen and I came to life! Now we have a team of sixteen oxen and horses. Daddy is famous because his oxen are so strong and pull all together just like one great strong ox.

Sometimes people even yell out PULL LIKE ONE and cheer when they see our team coming. They need us for sure.

Mister Moody and Mister Palmer brought their girls Ann Moody and Abigail Palmer along when they came. Ann's brother Harry came too. He could be a batboy for the baseball team soon. The mansion houses for important people like Mister Moody and Mister Palmer will get built first. John was at the bowling alley setting up the pins when they visited, so he did not meet them right then.

Oxen driver Felice Ariano and team

Ann said her mother, Clarissa Moody, used to be named Clarissa Jackling. She is the sister of the great Daniel C. Jackling—the leader of the whole project! Ann is very proud of her uncle D.C.

Mister Newton Baker is the Secretary of War for the United States of America. He is the man who named D.C. Jackling to be the leader of the government explosive plants.

Ann's uncle will rely a lot on Mister Moody. She said her whole family would live close to our farmhouse—this is TRUE. A month has gone by since then, and now I can walk right to her house on Twenty-First Street to see her.

The day I met Ann and Abigail I took them out to the stable to show them Mabel. She is a draft horse—people say she looks like a quarter horse because she has such strong hindquarters. She is roan with white fetlocks and feathers.

Local baseball team with batboy

Then we went across the field to the haybarn. Ann and Abigail were so surprised that we are allowed to climb up in the rafters and jump down into the hay. I took a pitchfork and fluffed up the hay so we could try it. We jumped over and over. Abigail got the idea to dig a tunnel under the hay—we laughed so hard. We bumped into each other in the tunnel because we were crawling around in the dark. I knew right then that we would be fast friends forever!

I wanted to have more fun so I went back to the house to ask Daddy if we could hitch Mabel up to the wagon and pull us around the field. Mister Moody said they had to leave, but maybe next time.

Abigail Palmer

At supper Daddy told us more about why Mister Moody and Mister Palmer came to see him. He had to explain to them about the different kinds of wood on the riverbanks. First-growth timber is very old, and very thick and strong. Oak is a hardwood and pine is a softwood. All these kinds of wood take a different amount of time to cut and haul. Daddy says George Washington surveyed this area in the Pocatalico Survey a long time ago, before we were even called the United States of America! The letters G and W are carved into a tree somewhere around here.

Daddy agreed to do the hauling.

They also asked Daddy if he could lay rails.

I know Daddy's face very well. It turned sad and worried when he said the men asked about it. He must have known something new was going to happen soon. Maybe he worried that our oxen and horses will not be needed as much in the future if there is a big train. Daddy and

Mother mostly live in the century that just ended. I am from the new century!

I want to tell them our old ways will never be lost. They will just be companions to help the new ways! Mother and Daddy will be important always. Horses are forever! I must find the perfect time to say this. I hope I can do it very soon.

Ann and Abigail will never have a horse. Their houses have maids who live in a special room in the basement—you cannot keep horses in a basement. They need pasture. Abigail's daddy told her motor cars and trains will become the most important soon. But I know for sure that old ways and new ways will always work together on everything.

I copied down this telegram Ann showed me from her uncle D.C. to her daddy:

> Drafting is underway for people ages 21–30. Could be 18–45. Possibility for industrial draft for munitions programs. Send all current plans and drawings. Must rely on married men and women. Executive houses planned prior. Meet specifications. D.C. JACKLING

My Plan

We have a new modern town name—Nitro. It is made from the word nitrocellulose.

Nitrocellulose is important for making gunpowder. It is also sometimes called gun cotton or flash paper. Those would be silly names for a town.

Somebody else wanted to name our town Redwop—powder spelled backwards—a horrible name for a town. I like Nitro the best. It sounds scientific.

Now that Ann and Abigail live here in Nitro I have made the perfect plan to help President Wilson win the war faster—it will take all three of us working together. I thought of it because Mother says writing down everything is very important. We will be a team of real war correspondents!

I read in school about the war correspondent Anna Steese Richardson. She is in France and is reporting from the trenches. I know that our President does not demand the war reports and pictures to be put out until we have won. But I think that would be too late! I think he is wrong about this. There—I wrote it down! I think he is wrong. I might mark this out later. But now that our gunpowder will blast the way to victory, we need to write reports to bring the President great comfort.

So here is my plan for Ann, Abigail, and me—and I have high hopes Elise and Emmaline will join in! We will send the President our own reports and pictures from here in Nitro. We are right on the scene. Ann and Abigail's daddies see everything first, so we are the best people for this job. Our village will go from farms to factories in only nine months. Two centuries will join together to win the Great War!

Farmland from then, and science from now.

VICTORY!

When we had to go to war, the President said Force, Force to the utmost, Force without stint or limit. This will inspire us while we work as correspondents!

We can do it. We will do it—we will not fail EVER. The riverbank is already cleared like our President ordered. In the picture we borrowed, you can see our farmhouse. Our nation and our town are moving forward to victory—I will report all about war work.

Cleared riverbank and doctors' houses

Here is my bold plan:

1. I will be the leader because this is all my idea.

2. I will pick the most important information.

3. Ann will pick out the science because her daddy is a chemical engineer. He has so much information to look at.

4. Abigail will pick the arithmetic because she is good at it.

5. We will name our reports *The Victory Chronicles*!

I will read to Ann and Abigail the letter President Wilson wrote to Miss Mildred White in Chambersburg in Pennsylvania. He calls her his little friend. He promises to do his best for all of us. This is pure proof children are important to him!

I copied the letter out from Missus Dudding. She says it is the real letter from a machine called a typewriter. Ann's daddy said their reports will be written using this new invention. This copied-out letter will be inspiration to write *The Victory Chronicles*! I hope Mildred White is twelve years old just like us. Maybe we will get our very own letter from the President!

Missus Zeins is another who wants to see the letter because she collects so many things. She has a banner made of silk with the words "Victory Sister" embroidered on it and golden fringe on the edges. She has lots of figurines and picture postcards of town. She says there will be lots of postcards now so everyone in Nitro can write about war progress.

There are so many rumors but that is not what *The Victory Chroni-cles* will be about. People spread so many rumors! Rumors like Missus

Woodrow Wilson is related to Pocahontas, or that people are dying from typhoid and typhoid inoculation in our new boomtown. We would never write about things like that. It would cause a panic.

WOODROW WILSON
us W. STATE ST., TRENTON, N. J.

November 13, 1912.

My dear little Friend:

I cannot tell you what gratification it gives me that you should think of me. Your letter has given me a great deal of genuine pleasure, and I hope that as the years go on you will continue to feel that I am the sort of man you would like to support and keep as your friend.

Cordially and faithfully yours,

Miss Mildred White,
        Chambersburg, Pa.

Letter from President Wilson to Miss Mildred White of Chambersburg, PA. For enlarged image, see Appendix.

We are called a boomtown now because so many people are coming so quickly. New men, new women and new families come with their trunks—some come with canvas bags over their shoulders. They are building houses for them and stores. It is all very exciting!

We can ask Mister Moody and Mister Palmer and all the scientists for facts—they have so much information they use for their reports. Those reports will be very important for future presidents to know how to make gunpowder quickly. They must let US use a few facts for *The Victory Chronicles.* Not too many—just enough for our *Victory Chronicles.*

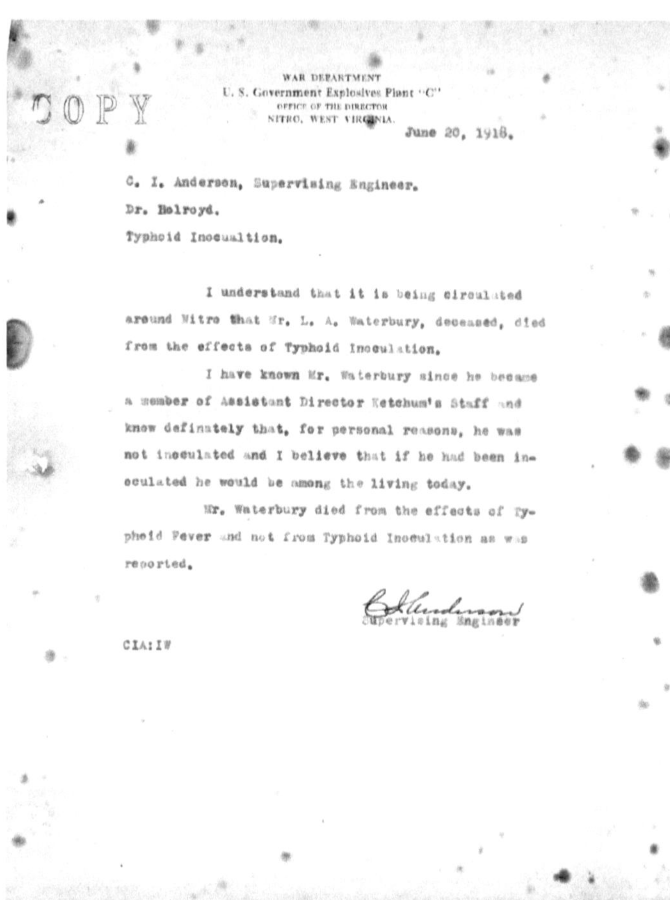

WAR DEPARTMENT
U. S. Government Explosives Plant "C"
OFFICE OF THE DIRECTOR
NITRO, WEST VIRGINIA.

June 20, 1918.

C. I. Anderson, Supervising Engineer.

Dr. Holroyd.

Typhoid Inocualtion.

I understand that it is being circulated around Nitro that Mr. L. A. Waterbury, deceased, died from the effects of Typhoid Inoculation.

I have known Mr. Waterbury since he became a member of Assistant Director Ketchum's Staff and know definately that, for personal reasons, he was not inoculated and I believe that if he had been inoculated he would be among the living today.

Mr. Waterbury died from the effects of Typhoid Fever and not from Typhoid Inoculation as was reported.

Supervising Engineer

CIA:IW

Letter from Plant C Supervising Engineer finding that Nitro resident died of typhoid fever, not as a result of typhoid inoculation

President Wilson will say to us directly: These reports are of great importance to me personally and to history.

Our work will be an inspiration for everyone. This is my personal challenge! I know Mother will probably read this, and I hope she does not say I am getting above my raising. I will tell her it is so important to perform your duties for America every day.

Writing to President Wilson!

February 8, 1918—we will write our dates just like they write in the reports—from now on and forever!

I am sitting down this morning to write my first letter to President Wilson. I am so excited that my hand is trembling. My letter to President Wilson goes like this:

Dear Mister President Woodrow Wilson,

I am Ana Ariano, age twelve. Ann Moody is my fast friend. Abigail Palmer is my next fast friend. We live right here in Nitro, West Virginia, where a miracle is happening! We promise we can make our share of five hundred thousand pounds of gunpowder every day to fight the Germans just like you ordered. So, we are growing a new century right out of our village farms—and we are doing it fast. We will not fail—not ever. Cross our hearts and hope to die. The riverbanks are already cleared just like you ordered. You can see our farm in the picture.

We understand that you do not want to see complete records and pictures of our huge war work until the

United States has won the war. But we want to help now! So, we will send you urgent reports and pictures along the way. We know this will help you bring about fast victory for America. We are naming our reports *The Victory Chronicles*. We will be your war correspondents! I am willing to offer my knowledge. This will be important war work. Gunpowder will blast the way to victory!

We are going to be a big help. I will send a picture of us—children who want to help. We even have a photographer here in town already. We have greatest confidence in you and the fighting soldiers and everybody else who is working for victory.

It is also very important for you to remember that my daddy is the best oxen driver of all. We are so happy to use our team to hurry up victory. The supply of oxen is large here. We have seventy-two. I can even tell you other places to buy them nearby like in Ohio—I can send you a picture of my favorite ox too. I named him Circle C for Explosives Plant C, which we are already building fast. I have a picture of all of us helpers—in Nitro we are a team for VICTORY!

By the way, Miss Etta Wilson says that she is your cousin. She lives close by in Milton, West Virginia. She has a picture postcard from you that says you could hardly hear her when you talked on the telephone after you got elected President. She showed it to everybody in the executive dining room at the new plant. But I worry this is just rumor. I do not want to put any rumors in our chronicles. That would not help our cause. So be sure to let me know if this is true.

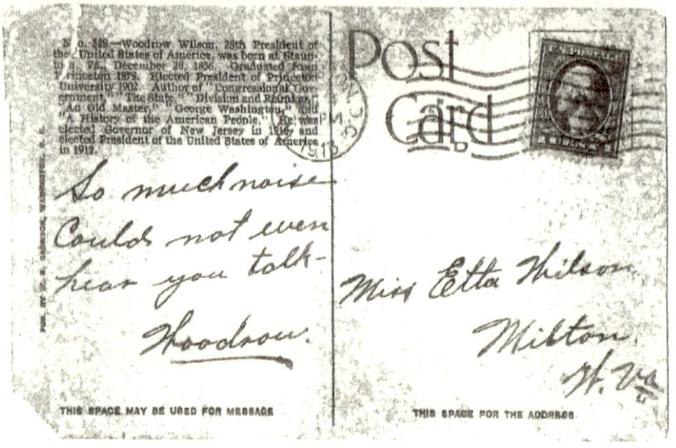

Postcard to Miss Etta Wilson

I am going to report everything—the good and the bad—even though I am dreading the bad!

Signed your True Reporters Sir,
Ana Ariano, Ann Moody, and Abigail Palmer

French postcard showing President Woodrow Wilson

The Champion Horses

February 12, 1918

It is true. We must work hard on transportation problems. Everybody is right—we do not have enough horses here. Valiant horses will always be needed. They are very brave and beautiful. They have to wear gas masks when they go to war, because of mustard gas and blistering agents. We will put this in our reports when we remember.

In Nitro the supervisors need good saddle horses because some of them ride to the plant from far away every day. And when they get here, we have almost two thousand acres of space—so the superintendents need horses to ride from one end of the plant to the other. We also have four hundred horses for patrols. We now have four stables spread around the plant. Just like all of the new workers coming to our new town, the horses need a place to live. The temporary stables were built in just one day on the sixth of January. It was just two weeks after the first engineers got here in December last year.

Horses equal speed! Everybody in Nitro rides, and my family are all very good riders, but we do not brag. We know the great importance of horses—and never doubt it.

Mister Samuel Hart is in charge of bringing the animals to the animal hospitals if they get sick, and sometimes he has extra horses to sell—really fine saddle horses. But we really need horses—we definitely do not have extras to sell! Is he a horse thief?

Just in January, so many horses have had to go to the hospital. Mister Hart says maybe one thousand will need to go before the war is over. The Stable Management Department told him that by the end of the war emergency more than ten million pounds of oats will be used. Maybe Abigail can do the arithmetic to figure out how many horseshoes that makes. Ha Ha. When they shoe the horses, they clean and trim the hooves. I know all about taking care of horses.

Riders at Plant C

With all these horses, they are going to build three more animal hospitals—each one with a veterinarian doctor. We will help find horses to send to the soldiers in Europe—war horses! Sometimes the horses have to stay here for a while first, because they are green or get sick. Then they are broken to the saddle, the bridle and the reins. I heard we now have two thousand draft horses and mules—five hundred saddle horses and seventy-two head of oxen. Some of them have to be rented. But somebody else told us that twenty-five thousand horses will be needed. The numbers are confusing.

A team was just sent to New York to buy more animals. We bought three mules from Saint Louis in Missouri, and we are going to get more later from Ohio—last time we only bought six oxen. This seems like a low number to me because I know the oxen are needed for work here in our boomtown.

I hope everybody at the plant knows the different ways to cool down the horses after riding. This is very important. It is especially important to give the horses alfalfa, which is good for energy—like a tonic. Our horses need energy for all the work.

Pay wagon

We will borrow the picture of the police patrol horse and rider for our *Victory Chronicles*. We will put it back after only one day. I heard there are also horses pulling pay wagons to carry more than four hundred thousand dollars every Friday morning. The wagons have watchguards, but I cannot believe they have to carry all that money around to pay the workers. But there are around eighteen thousand workers now at the plants. It is so scary to have all that money on a wagon!

We asked Daddy if there was a chance that we could buy Big Red from the Critchfield farm—he said no because Big Red killed a man once.

Saddle tank switch engine

Ann's daddy says that motorcars and trains will soon become the most important part of transportation—more important than horses and oxen. But when I have children, I will make sure they know how to ride—and ride very well at that. Our farm has an oak tree with a branch that makes a perfect saddle to show children how to ride. My future husband will have to love horses! Ann and Abigail and Elise and Emmaline only have enough land for a victory garden. I am so lucky to live on a farm.

I borrowed pictures of so many different horses that pass across our farm. I hope Daddy is not too upset about what Ann's daddy said. Horses are still at the top, but motorcars and trains matter too! Daddy does not like it when we talk about things like the saddle tank switch engine!

Here is what I say—steam locomotives will never steam past horses! My word joke.

Assets and
Resources

Many were accused of hindering the war effort, including David Lamar, who was accused of delaying munitions production by urging strikes. For enlarged image, see Appendix.

Noble Carter wants to be friends. He is just such a fussbudget! He thinks that the river patrols are not policemen or rum runners but spies who steal things and escape down the river. He showed us some spy pictures—including one of David Lamar from New York. He has a big thick mustache and a straw hat. He tried to stop munitions with strike plots and is now in prison for one year.

For our *Victory Chronicles*, we made a list of our assets for the President:

1. We are mainly farmers and so we have farmhouses that are acres apart from each other. This is important for safety where gunpowder is being made and tested—it takes a lot of space. We are a village with nine hundred people—last year we were only seventy-five! And we are still growing fast. Soon we will be a big town like Charleston—they have a railroad!

2. They say we have an abundance of natural resources.

3. Our valley has a wonderful river—very wide and very deep. It almost never freezes over. It is called Great Kanawha River.

4. We have plenty of trees—important for building the railbeds and houses. The riverbank is already cleared like you ordered.

5. Soon we will have a cotton bale house so we can get plenty of cotton—very important for making gunpowder.

6. We have plenty of workmen for all three work shifts. Daddy will work the day shift from seven in the morning until four in the afternoon—hooray! Because our oxen cannot work at nighttime. Two more shifts mean that the plant will be working all around the clock. The men have to share their beds. Missus Hayes says her beds have lice!

7. No criminals are allowed to work at the plant.

8. They are working on emergency electric in case there is ever a fire near the gunpowder and the power breaks down. Daddy heard this at Sigmon's restaurant—he goes there to get the news from the other shifts.

9. We have plenty of coal to be mined, plus gas and salt. Everybody brags about this.

10. We have the famous Kanawha-Michigan rail line. They are laying new tracks close to Main Street.

11. We have a growing village of people who are all so proud to help America win the war!

Explosives Plant C ammunition testing grounds

We meet up at Ann's house to work on our *Victory Chronicles* for President Wilson. I cannot tell my sister Sarah about our work because she tells everything she hears and listens to rumors and gets scared. Ann's house is very beautiful, but all her brother Harry cares about is his pet black snake named Bart.

PRIVATE: I am worried—Mother and I are becoming jealous of modern ways. I admit I want a telephone. VERY PRIVATE: Mother—if you are reading this, do not spread around the rumor about typhoid fever here in Nitro! Everyone will panic!

Information for the Victory Chronicles

February 26, 1918

Ann's uncle D.C. is the head of all the plants and has something called an administration chart—lists all the important people with information about the war effort. Daddy's name is on the chart! Maybe we should borrow it for a day or two so that we know who can answer our questions for the *Victory Chronicles*.

Noble Carter sitting on the porch of a bungalow

Noble Carter's daddy is Dwight Carter—a carpenter. He makes sure that the ammunition boxes are perfect and will be ready to go out on time. Sometimes he works as a mechanic at all the different plants. We think Noble will have some information about the war effort for us.

We call Noble Chip because he whittles sticks all the time with his penknife. He does this to make whistles. Last Saturday, Abigail asked him right out if he would help us. She is so bold that she even promised him a kiss on the lips! He said he wanted more than that, and he meant the kind of thing Ann's mother knows about from nursing. Ann got so mad and wanted to tell Noble's mother what he said, but that might not be a good idea because we still need information from him about his daddy's work. So we did not tell on him.

Nitric acid at Explosives Plant C

We decided we really hate Noble, but we love his dog Bunkhouse. We found a picture of him on the porch with Bunkhouse. Our new friend Ivy lives across the street from Noble.

We know what the inside of Noble's house looks like because we saw all the house plans. His house is plan number 175. His bedroom is one hundred square feet, but in the plans for the mansion houses where Ann and Abigail live the bedrooms have only eighty-five square feet—so there can be room for their maids to sleep.

Andrew Hutchinson

Andrew Hutchinson tells lies all of the time. Today after school let out he told me every one of the boys has the most important drawings of the ammunition boxes to study. He had a piece of paper but would not show me. He said it was the secret plan for the nitric acid plant he found when he snuck past the guards after the end of the second shift. He says there are huge and dangerous vats. He told me the acid looks like big piles of snow and that he made a snow angel in it. No—he did not! Nitric acid is very dangerous. Boys are so annoying.

Devil Duster

March 5, 1918

All the girls were completely humiliated in front of everybody today.

Missus Marsh told us we had to square dance. We gathered around in a circle and had to hold hands with the boys. When she went to get the triangle to make music Kevin Hartman yelled out that he saw the devil in the plant.

I saw him, I did! The head guard took me into the devil duster area right after the whistle blew to end the first shift, he said exactly. The devil was back in a dark corner with a cloud of powder spraying all over his face and arms but the devil disappeared in a giant puff before he said anything.

We called him a great big liar!

Before Missus Marsh came back, Kevin took a picture out of his book satchel and showed it to everyone. It said Devil Duster at the bottom. All the boys stomped their feet and hooted at us for calling him a liar! After that we did not have any fun square dancing. We should have told on them.

Bucky said You do not know nothing, no way, no how! He even talks wrong.

Noble and Andrew and Kevin and Bucky are the stupidest boys in the world.

Kevin Hartman

Secret Letters

March 8, 1918

Noble handed Abigail and Ann and me a secret letter today. He never gives up! He signed the letter SP for Special Project. He wants us to meet him at Mister McCallister's pet store on Tenth Street at six o'clock tomorrow night. It has something to do with the *Chronicles*, but he said there was true danger now.

You must come—this is very serious. That is what the note said.

The pet store is where we play spotlight at night when it is not muddy. Emmaline has a flashlight and the one who is IT shines it around to spotlight somebody who is hiding out. That person is IT if they get caught. It is fun, but Elise and Emmaline are so mean. One time Emmaline pinched me on the arm so that I would scream and get spotlighted. I did not scream—I just pinched her right back. But then she pulled on my hair, so I went to trip her, but my feet rustled the leaves around. We both got spotlighted and Emmaline made me be IT.

Ann thinks Noble's note is just a trick, but Abigail and I are kind of thinking that we should go. I am a little afraid that Noble just wants to hurt our feelings—but if it is a trick, we will get him right back!

Ivy told Ann that Noble's daddy yells a lot. People call him Grain Man. The ambulance wagon goes right down his street. We have to decide if we will meet him. Tonight I will bring Mabel in from the pasture and study my lessons.

The Pet Store

March 9, 1918

The three of us did go to meet Noble after all. We zig-zagged between the railroad tracks and down the road to the pet store. Noble came, looking around all the time like he thought maybe we had not come, or that we were followed. He has called us scaredy cats before, but he is the one who looked scared.

Telephone operators at Explosives Plant C

He started off in a very mean way.

I feel sorry for you he said, and I hate your stupid games. But then he got real quiet and told us again his mother is a telephone operator.

She hears a lot of things.

He said there could be forest fires when the leaves fall. That was scary. Then he said the most horrible thing of all—war profiteers might murder us if we do not stop what we are doing here in Nitro!

The war profiteers are everywhere—then Noble was done talking and quick as lightning he ran away through the barberry bushes so we could not follow him.

I walked home in the dark over the tracks and past the acid plant. My mind was twirling around in circles. Should we report this to President Wilson?

Mother thinks castor oil solves every problem—a dose of that nasty stuff cannot help me now.

First Mistake?

March 13, 1918

I am writing this at half past seven in the evening, and I am very tired. Today we had to make an outline of another map from page thirteen of our *School History of The Great War* book. We had to outline all the regions Germany wants to conquer. I am so tired of having to read all this extra information about the war. I feel confused and angry and scared almost all of the time—I try not to show it.

President Wilson created the Committee on Public Information to give everybody in America important facts about the war. I need to organize all the important information I have learned, but I hate to make outlines! I am worried we will have to make so many outlines for our *Chronicles*. Poor me! Poor Ann! Poor Abigail! There are so many facts for us to put in order.

Even Ann's daddy is having trouble writing up his own reports because there is so much information coming to his desk. He says it is all getting mixed up and some of it is missing. Ann said that he was very mad at her mother last night and even yelled at her. He probably said well my stars in heaven. That is what he says whenever he is mad. He worries a lot.

When we borrowed pictures from Ann's daddy's reports we saw that we had to fix a lot of numbers on the buildings they wrote down. We might need to make an outline to keep everything straight after all.

Abigail thinks it will be too hard to copy out all the documents and sums and averages and send pictures too. We already know that our government sent an official photographer to make pictures of this for all the reports. We will keep on sending the pictures anyway. The photographer might miss something important. After all—our pictures will let the President see our faces full of joy and no fear.

Administration Building at Plant C, later burned in suspicious fire

We even have a picture of the photographer loading his big glass negative into the camera to make a picture. And another picture shows the railroad tracks and our farm both at the same time. Two centuries in one picture!

I guess our *Victory Chronicles* should have started with the contract signed by Mister D.C. Jackling—President Wilson already knows all about that. Everyone in Nitro should already know about it. We cannot wait until the war is over to put everything in order and send to

President Wilson. We are here every day—we will be here on Victory Day—it does not make sense to wait for victory. We will send all the plans that we know NOW.

Wartime photographer

I must be bold like Ann and ask politely about the new modern school we will be getting. Please give me courage!

Railroad tracks with farm in the background

Here goes my outline of what to write in our *Victory Chronicles*. The night is long but I will write it out if it takes me until the sun comes up!

1. We copied down as many of the names of all the buildings that will be built as we could. There are so many that we could not copy down all of them, and we had to fix some of the numbers on our list again because they were still wrong. The mistakes have all been fixed now.

2. We have excellent resources—a big river—lots of land—plenty of coal and gas and timber. This will bring great comfort to President Wilson.

3. People come here to work from many countries—they want

to help in this emergency. There are more Italian people here now, not just us Arianos.

4. There is a brand-new job called industrial nursing.

5. New hospitals!

6. The science for making gunpowder—sulfuric acid must be heated way up.

7. In another *Chronicle* it will be the time to write about the big parades of American pride.

8. We should write about houses first or maybe transportation—houses are built so fast. Transportation is going so fast too—we will have to borrow some train maps.

9. One meeting happened in February in the big city of Philadelphia. Important people from New York were there, too.

10. Daddy says someone named Mister Samuel Gompers is working for workers. This is important.

11. There is a Department of Housing in Washington, D.C. I am sure President Wilson knows about this already, but we must include everything in our *Victory Chronicles*.

12. Horse patrols keep us safe. If there really are any enemy incursions, we even have police patrols on the river. Noble calls them crooks—I will not write that!

I do worry we will lose track of some of our information. There is so much! Some of it is starting to confuse us. But I will write the *Victory Chronicles* and make sure not to leave anything out. I will not lose my courage. I promise myself!

Police patrol boat

DO THIS ANA: Send a *Victory Chronicle* to thank President Wilson for all the wonderful new things we have here—music concerts, boxing, a bowling alley, a dairy and even a meat market. We will not have to think about the war so much with all these new things! I must also be bold like Abigail and find a polite way to ask about the new modern school we will be getting.

I am going to sleep now. Give me courage!

Saturday

*M**arch 16, 1918*

Today is Saturday. My chores were finished by eleven o'clock—hooray! I took Mother's basket of sewing scraps to Ivy's house. We planned to make doll clothes out of remnants and bits of lace and other trims. My doll Marion was going to get a new dress with a lace collar. But when I got to Ivy's house she took me to the front room to peek across the street.

I knew why right away—Noble's house is over there.

Noble's house had a broken window in the front, and the curtains were hanging outside the broken window. They were pretty curtains white like clouds, but it was all wrong that they were outside! Ivy said that the ambulance wagon took somebody to the plant hospital yesterday afternoon.

I got very worried and felt that Ivy and I needed to go over there and find out what had happened. As much as I hate Noble, I do not want him to have bad fortune. And Noble's daddy is very important in the war effort—he must not get hurt. At this critical time everybody must stay well.

Ivy's mother was talking on the telephone about the ambulance wagon when we came back into the kitchen. We heard her say little pitchers have big ears. Then she stopped.

She meant us!

Ivy's real name is Iva, and she is becoming a dear friend to me. I like calling her Ivy. I like endearing nicknames—not cruel ones. One of Ivy's neighbors has the nickname of Hatrack because he does not work very hard at the plant.

Noble's daddy's Dwight goes to have rhubarb wine with Daddy and the other men on Saturdays. I heard a man at the Lock 7 store say that Dwight sure does not listen to the urgent call to save grain for the horses. I think he was talking about liquor. That is why they call Dwight Grain Man.

I can only pray that the ambulance wagon visit was just a rumor I heard. I do not want this rumor to get to President Wilson and make him get discouraged.

Bevo

Daddy drinks one Bevo soft drink every night. And every night he says milk or water might have bacteria, but Bevo never does. I already know this, because I see it all the time in Mother's *Woman's Home Companion* magazine. We get the magazines because Mother is a subscriber. She keeps them away out of sight so that Daddy does not know she gets magazines. Mother keeps secrets!

At supper tonight Mother told us again how much she would like to be a subscriber to *The Delineator*. That is the magazine that had the story about Brave Little Belgium.

She said it is so sad that we cannot spend even one dollar a month for enlightenment.

We listened again to her telling how Beatty let her copy out information from the magazine on how to save one dollar every month by selling subscriptions to *Woman's Home Companion*. Daddy just shook his head and wanted me or Ellen to get him one more Bevo and bring it to the table.

I hate all the broccoli and squash we eat for supper from Mother's victory garden, even when she promises that it is from a recipe for French Culinary Delight. Well, the day was over when Daddy grinned and said that he was very sad because we could not afford three hundred and sixty-five dollars for an electric Victrola. He laughed and got up to leave the table.

I believe Mother always keeps lots of secrets.

Mister Thomas Marshall is the Vice President of the United States of America and he wrote a story called "An Ideal Marriage" in *Woman's Home Companion*. In my perfect marriage of the future I will marry someone like Mister Thomas Marshall. He believes that no man should spend even a dollar on himself unless his wife has an equal amount. He believes marriage should be a partnership! I bet Mister and Missus Marshall are very happy. Mother and Daddy have to talk about money all the time. Should I tell them what Mister Marshall thinks? I am not sure.

I like to read the magazines—one thing I do NOT like is when people make stories in the magazines about the kind of work women should do. All the work is important to me—a man's work or a woman's work. I hope that the magazine's editors know that.

NOT FOR PRESIDENT WILSON'S EYES: I feel very awful tonight, and I just keep writing on and on. Everybody thinks we are still babies. But it is wartime and we are growing up pretty fast. Ann knows a lot of grown-up facts. She knows about cocktails. She told me about a cocktail called the French 75. It is named after the Howitzer 75mm gun, which fires a lot of ammunition very fast. She says that it only takes .07 seconds.

Ann's parents drink cocktails with important people. Everybody—even the children—knows that cocktails are not really allowed because we need all the grain we can get to feed the animals and soldiers in the war. But cocktails are not against the law. I know myself about rhubarb wine. It is made in Blakes Creek Valley. I know for sure that no animal feed can be made from rhubarb so rhubarb wine is alright.

Sometimes we eat rhubarb pie. It turns kind of pink and slides out of the crust. Rhubarb cobbler in a bowl is better.

I really am getting confused about what to write down.

Here is something I am thinking about tonight—Daddy is worried about our oxen team. I was surprised when he said that only six had been purchased lately for hauling. The steam locomotives will steam right over the oxen haulers soon. I did not think so when I made my word joke—but now I think it could really happen. Daddy is starting to study train engines now. I think he is afraid he will not have any modern work to do on account of the trains. I am afraid of so many things now but I try to hide it. But most of all I do not like seeing Daddy afraid.

And that is my report for today!

Missus Funston's Advice

*M**arch 22, 1918*

Mother keeps telling me I must be prepared for the new modern school when it opens. I know this. I also know very well that I must keep on being a war correspondent to President Wilson—I can study everything together.

Mother saves all her secret magazines. Sometimes they come late because of the wartime traffic.

She made a list of everything I must read before she makes me a new school dress:

1. "Molly Make-Believe," "White Linen Nurse," and "Old-Dad," all by Eleanor Abbott

2. Anna Steese Richardson is a war correspondent sending reports from the war zone in France—just like me.

3. Margaret Deland writes stories in the magazines.

4. Grace Gould writes about fashion.

5. "Tower-Room Talks" by Ann Bryan McCall

There is a lady named Missus Funston—gives out advice for mothers and wives and sisters and sweethearts—all about the knitting teas to knit socks and sweaters for the soldiers. Some soldiers do not even have shoes. Men and women and children are all knitting socks and sweaters. Mother knits socks and sweaters. But Missus Funston says do not go to the knitting teas if there is too much gossip.

Miss Gould's fashion advice in Woman's Home Companion,
September 1918

Missus Funston is very upset when women talk about the horrors of the war. Her husband is Mister Funston—named Fighting General Funston.

Do not talk so much! Missus Funston tells us this. It hinders the soldiers.

She is totally disgusted with war profiteering—she says we must make the best of it. We have to make do! She goes on and on.

Mrs. Frederick Funston

I cannot knit and purl to help the war effort because I am left-handed. Elise and Emmaline are such bullies about it—keep telling me they will miss me a lot in heaven and hope there is not too much fire where I have to go.

I wish Missus Funston could know somehow that we are keeping our spirits high. Nobody complains too much. I do not think I need more advice about wartime and I know Ann and Elise and Emmaline would not like it—they are bolder than I am.

I promised Mother I would read "Tower-Room Talks" by Ann Bryan McCall. She encourages girls to develop and train our powers if we are to be worthy of the stupendous times we live in. She tells girls to understand the importance of memory. Her own mother committed famous poems to memory. But memory is important in a different way now. Today, in 1918, memory should be a partner with importance. These are important times, and memories are friends, not servants.

In this time of war, when we all must do our part, we are creating far more important memories than those that are used just to perform bare memory feats. I will remember everything in our *Victory Chronicles,* because it is all written down.

I am excited about the smart ideas I found in Mother's newest magazine. I might try to enter the contests. We can send in a picture of our pet. I might send a picture of Circle C or Mabel to the Secretary for *Woman's Home Companion* in New York City. I borrowed the picture—might win the one-dollar prize money—they might even put the pictures in the magazine. There is a rhyme contest too.

The subject of the rhyme contest is "The Story of the Thrift Stamp." That might be too hard for me. I explained to Ivy that a rhyme is kind of like a song. For the story contest, the subject is "Stay at Home Fun."

I think my story about all the fun we have in the haybarn might win a prize. Here are the rules for the stories:

1. Original (do not copy)

2. Only write on one side of the paper

3. Do not roll up the paper

4. Age limit is twelve years old

centuries—this new one and the old one—try to get extra money from this war emergency instead of working hard for victory. It gives me hateful thoughts. I have to get in my bed to go to sleep.

***

Now I am awake again—still thinking about all kinds of scary things like how coyotes steal chickens and chicks or sometimes even a foal. Foals do not know how to run away even when coyotes are close by. Coyotes get together in packs and run together all day and all night. A big one carried off Elise's cat last week. She even saw it happen—her screams could not stop it. Coyotes woke me up just now—I am sure of it. But that is alright because I was having a nightmare. When I woke up there were tears down my cheeks. I hope I was not screaming out to wake everybody up. I do not think so because nobody came to find out about me.

My dream started out when I went into our school on the very first day. The American flag was high on a pole. I had a new dress with furbelows. I looked around for my desk, but the desks were all shaped wrong for me because I write with my left hand, so I have to turn my paper backwards. There was an inkwell on the desk to hold lots of ink—I was very happy.

But then a great wind blew our new schoolteacher in through the door, and it was none other than Missus Funston! She looked just like her picture in Mother's magazine and she pulled a ferocious coyote out of her pocketbook.

Speak out of turn once, and I will send him straight down the row to you! She looked around the room and pointed her bony finger at me.

You will never have a special desk just because you write with your left hand. I hate it when pupils ask questions. She kept pointing right at me—YOU! Did you read my advice in the magazine?

I was glad right then that Mother made me read it two times. I stood up beside my desk and gave the proper definition of war profiteering, which I did very clearly and well. But it was not good enough for Missus Funston!

She took my slate and drew a big circle on it—told me to put my nose inside the circle until I can answer the question.

My mind was racing, and my heart was pounding. It felt like I had my nose in there for a whole hour before I remembered something Abigail said.

A very good friend told me that people can change up the sums of money numbers to get extra money from the war emergency, I said that exactly to Missus Funston. It is very bad.

Missus Funston must have given up on me then because she told Karen Kay to stand up and recite a better answer. But Donny had tied her dress sash to the back of her seat so when she tried to stand up she fell right back down.

Sic Donny! Missus Funston yelled out and set her coyote free and pointed right at Donny. The coyote ran straight toward his seat and began to roll back its lip to show huge black teeth.

All of a sudden Mayor Daniels jumped out of the coat closet where he was hiding. He was there to save us! No—he picked me up by the arm and took me away and pulled me all along Fourth Street to the jail.

A lot of people were waiting for us when we got to the jail. They pointed at me and barked—just like coyotes!

Did you send a *Chronicle* to President Wilson with important sums?

Did you write about spending one million dollars on platinum?

Hatrack was asleep in a jail cell. I did not know he was a criminal. There were ten jail cells for men and three for women. While they locked me up I could hear Missus Funston's voice—if you ever forget about war profiteering, you will be held back one grade! I cried and cried. If I got held back, I could never be a famous writer. Right then I woke up! I might never go back to sleep in my life.

Really, it is no wonder I have nightmares, the way Mother behaves—tonight she cooked cucumbers with squash and piled plain old breadcrumbs on top.

We must not eat food that should be sent to our soldiers who are fighting the Germans every day—she went on and on.

Now I am not complaining about eating food from our victory garden. I know we must save food for our soldiers. Food is ammunition, do not waste it! I read that. I am getting suspicions. How could people be making money for themselves in this emergency war project? Are they holding back food? I cannot ask Mother about that—I am afraid and angry most of the time about this—I do not want to ask anybody for answers.

Noble says that people have been murdered trying to find out the whole truth—not just one person—many. His mother is a real telephone operator, so she hears all sorts of things, but I do not know if that explains why Noble tells me these horrible things. This gives me a stomachache. Or maybe it is just all the cucumbers.

I cannot sleep, so I will study more about war profiteering so our *Victory Chronicles* can be even more correct. I do hope we cannot get in trouble just because some of them got lost or sent out. It does not count as a lie if sometimes we send out wrong reports. We are just copying down what we see.

I will sit at my desk and study war profiteering like Missus Funston talked about.

War profiteering:
People ask for extra money, much more than they need. That means they are stealing things. The crimes are secret, of course, and hard to find out about. But asking for too much money means that some money is going to the war profiteers in secret. Why does Mister Hart sell some of our horses? Is he a horse thief?

I am so mad at myself now.
GO BACK TO SLEEP, ANA!
But I cannot.
I hope and pray that our *Chronicles* are safe with President Wilson and the United States Secretary of War. His name is Mister Newton Baker—he is from West Virginia, just like me. They say he selected General Pershing himself to lead the American Expeditionary Forces, but I do not know for sure, so I better not report on that.

We can never tell anyone—even our daddies—about exactly what is in our *Victory Chronicles* until the war is over. It is too risky.

Is Noble telling the truth or is he just trying to scare us with his crazy ideas about lies and money? Abigail is no help. Her numbers are too confusing. First she told me that the war would cost fifty million dollars but now she says seven hundred and seventy million dollars. Can this be true?

I must go to sleep.

Coal, Power, Electricity, and Murder

April 2, 1918

A I wrote an unforgettable statement for the next *Victory Chronicle*: If horses are the past, and locomotives are the future, coal is now.

Coal power is the key for Plant C. We need a powerhouse and a boiler house—the main bases for the steam, compressed air and electric for the plant. That means we need an electric transformer bank, too. Ann said that she would explain compressed air to me at a later time.

For locomotives, the six-wheel switch engine is very important because a lot of train cars have to be switched around. They will need two thousand feet of railroad tracks just to turn them around. There are steam locomotives of narrow gauge, and some of standard gauge. I do not understand the difference—Daddy will.

There is something else important called the saddle tank switch engine to move things around, and for low-speed work to go short distances. Engines will pull hopper cars, side-dumping cars, and flat cars. Flat cars are very important. All of our explosive supplies have to come in on the flat cars, and the gunpowder ammunition has to sent out to war on flat cars in strong boxes.

Flat cars for transport

Abigail said an average of two hundred fifty trains will come every day. We copy everything down now just like it is in the reports. She said her arithmetic told her this—but now she says it could be five thousand trains every day. The rest of us get so angry with her when she mixes up the numbers! It will be our duty to count all the trains. We must make sure that the trains work their way all the way through Plant C—all the way through the hospitals, the powerhouse, the boiler house, the box shop, the cotton bale house, the new dairy—so many more stops! Even the stables. The war emergency has put every train to work every day.

The way to victory is clear—coal, horses, trains, scientists, farmers, and people from all over the world working together! Two centuries at once!

I am so worried all the time about Noble's rumors about war profiteering and even murder. I can think of all kinds of ways to murder war correspondents like us. I even made a list!

1. The coal goes to the unloading trestle, which can carry seventy-five thousand tons of coal. The trestle is six hundred fifty feet long. The locomotive cranes lift the coal into the hopper. **We could be thrown into the hopper!**

2. After the coal is dumped into the hopper, it gets crushed and goes through the coal scrubber. **We could be crushed in the hopper!**

3. The coal fires up the boilers to send out the power. Dry saturated steam—whatever that is—very important. I heard that we can make at least one thousand pounds of steam every hour. **We could be burned up in the boiler the way Mother's canner uses steam!**

4. At the very end, the ash-dumping cars carry the cinders away. They must keep water in the ash tunnel to keep it wet when the cinders go through it. We have a lot of deep wells here to supply the water. **We could be drowned in the ash tunnel!**

5. **We could be packed away in the ammunition boxes leaving Plant C!** But this does not have to mean murder. If we got packed up—I hope we would get sent to France. If we escape in France we can thank all the French people for their hard work before we come home. And we could go to Brave Little Belgium and Britain. I would like to learn how to say thank you in French.

There are so many ways we could be murdered by the war profiteer criminals. They would do anything to keep their secrets—like throw us in the acid tanks. I can feel my legs burning just thinking about it. Daddy says that many acids are dangerous—especially sulfuric acid. Sometimes I feel like acid is seeping into my brain and burning it up.

Transformer bank at Explosives Plant C

We borrowed the electric supply map. I hope there is not anything secret on it. There are four electric transformer banks with six thou-sand volts of electric. If we touch that it would kill us for sure!

So many dangerous possibilities—I feel like I will never live long enough to go to the new school or play spotlight in the summer or see victory in the war. I will not be alive to get a Brownie Box camera for Christmas and use it for war work. And poor Mother will feel so awful if I am murdered! I love her so much. She is never sneaky the way she says children can be—except when she does not tell Daddy about her magazines. I hope Sarah and Ellen and John will take good care of Mabel and Circle C when I am gone. Maybe I will tell Ann and Abigail about my fears before my mind speeds away.

***

We met up a few hours ago while the sun was still shining. I do not think anybody saw us because the Joe Pye Weeds grow high in the field and their fuzzy purple flowers could hide us. The field is very close to the ice plant where people get their ice blocks or send them out places—like Plant C. I told Ann and Abigail about caustic soda—can make you go blind even if it looks just like sugar. How can I worry about taking the wash off the clothesline with such dangers around us?

But Ann and Abigail did not start crying when I told them death could come in one of many horrible ways in the tunnel.

I will carry a small garden shovel with me always in case we get buried in Mister Muck's tunnel—from Abigail.

And I will hide water in my satchel to cure caustic soda burns—from Emmaline.

I am lucky to have such bold friends!

We will be on the lookout for the spies from the pictures Noble showed us. I feel much better now. We will ask Noble for some of the whistles that he makes so we can make loud sounds to warn each other of danger.

All the new houses here will get electric. Even our farmhouse will get electric because we gave up some of our pastures for the railbeds. We like electric but we are happy to help any way we can. We are so proud that our West Virginia coal is such a strong weapon for war! Daddy says we will not get a radio just because we get electric—radio waves are needed for the soldiers!

Soldiers' barracks at Explosives Plant C

West Virginia Coal

*A**pril 9, 1918*

Dear Mister President Wilson Sir,

Our workers are very diligent and eager to work hard here in Nitro, but we do not yet have enough workers here to supply our great needs. So, special passenger trains will bring even more workers to Plant C. The trains will pick up people in Charleston, West Charleston, Dunbar, Institute, and Sattes. There is no bus to bring workers here because our roads are very bad. The trains will have fourteen coaches. The fare started out at sixteen cents for a one-way ride—now it costs more. My daddy could work as the man who collects fares on the train. This could be his new modern work if they do not want our oxen anymore.

I hear there will be five thousand train riders every day until we win the war. These terrible war conditions mean that all the trains must run every day—also ferry rides down the Great Kanawha River. We mostly use trains because many supplies cannot come by water. Coal can come down the river, so we can send power out fast! Everything is moving so fast—from farms to factories to war.

It will be necessary to run train tracks all the way around the plant. I have heard eighteen thousand feet and fifty-three miles of train track. Those are different. Which one is right? I think these numbers are wrong because someone was counting the miles in the trip going back too for the passenger trains. But the trains use the same railroad tracks to go both ways! We will have to get to the bottom of this.

The trains must go all the way around the plant and also to the hospitals, the powerhouse, the boiler house, and the boxhouse. The boxhouse is where they make the boxes for the ammunition. The tracks will even go by the stables! People will surely complain if the trains do not go everywhere they are needed.

We will observe and report back to you. This war emergency puts everything and everyone to work every day.

Signed real war correspondents,
Ana, Ann, and Abigail

PRIVATE: I would like to tell President Wilson I believe in the future of trains—but I mostly believe in horses. I know oxen could not pull as many cars the way a locomotive can. Mother and Daddy will have to find other important work. Ann and Abigail do not always understand how important it is to me for both centuries to be working at the same time. Mother and Daddy see the future coming—they worry about it—and think there will be not be a place for them in this new century.

I should start a *Victory Chronicle* like this—our coal will always be a strong weapon for the whole world!

Everybody Goes to Charleston but Me

April 21, 1918

Plant C has a garage with sixty-four cars—thirty-seven touring cars and twenty-seven roadsters. There are forty-seven men to take care of the cars, and there are other workers to drive the cars. The cars are not supposed to leave the plant, but Ann and Abigail get to ride in one to Charleston today—sixteen miles away—because their daddies are very important there. They asked Elise and Emmaline to go with them, but not me. It makes me feel very sad.

I am left behind here to write a *Victory Chronicle* about all the new houses while they are gone. I do not even want to write about the houses. I wanted to send out our train map. We took a vote—Ann and Abigail voted together for houses. So I am up here in the hayloft now, with a corn snake sliding around in the logs bothering me with flashes of red and orange. Sarah always hides snakes in our hay tunnel.

Ann and Abigail and Elise and Emmaline all live on silk stocking row. It is called that because their houses are mansions, and they have Tarvia on their roads so there is no mud. They want me to put in a picture of their big houses in this *Victory Chronicle*. The mansions have eight rooms and a sunporch. There is a room for the maids in the basement, a trunk room, and an attic, too. The government even paid for fancy furniture in each house—two rugs, one bookcase, four rocking chairs, one wicker center table, one oak buffet, five straight-back chairs with leather seats, and one dining table. We do not have anything like that.

I will write about their fancy houses, but I promise I will write about the plain ones too—only fair! The plain houses only get one rug—cement floors—no basement. They do not get brick foundations. I need to borrow pictures of the houses for our *Victory Chronicles*. President Wilson will not have time to look at their fancy furniture anyway because he has a war to run.

Boarding house kitchen

All of the workers want a real house so their families can live with them. But we need so many houses, and lots of people leave after about forty-three days, So we build dormitories and boarding houses and bring in small houses by rail in different pieces. About one hundred eighty people can live in the lodging buildings. They all work together and live together, just like the soldiers do! Sometimes people have to sleep in a basement, or in the attic so all the workers can fit in. Sometimes workers have to share their bed if they work on different shifts because they sleep at different times. Missus Hayes said her beds have lice in them.

Executive residence at Explosives Plant C

Making enough houses is a big problem. There was a meeting in Philadelphia in February about this. Missus John D. Rockefeller Junior was there for women, and Mister Gompers was there for the workers. Things are very worrisome for women. Many of the nurses have died in the war—mostly in France. I am hearing numbers from two hundred all the way to five hundred. Ann's mother is an industrial nurse, and she says there could be four thousand women workers here.

But I also heard that it is probably one thousand and a lot of them have to live in private homes. Two hundred fifty women will need company housing. Some will have to live in the new Young Women's Christian Association building.

Plan for skilled mechanic's bungalow

Abigail says that the six hundred fifty-seven bungalows cost five dollars each. Bigger houses cost a lot more money. The barracks for the soldiers and the executive houses are built first. The first house was built in only two days! I cannot believe Abigail left me to do all these sums by myself. Sometimes she is very cruel and says I am no good at arithmetic.

Here is my list:

- 657 bungalows—cost $5.00 each—I will write down costs like this so that it is like the reports.

- 4 company barracks—cost $250.00 each.

- 5 whole houses for chemists with families, plus around 50 more chemists who live in boarding houses.

- 100 houses with four rooms—cost $5.00 or $8.00 each.

- 20 houses with 5 rooms—cost $5.00 or $8.00 each. Somebody got numbers confused. Bigger houses cost a lot more money.

- Unskilled workers get 500 houses for white people—1,000 for colored people—908 for foreign people. Some of the houses are like two houses in one—sharing a kitchen and toilet room.

- Some houses are only for skilled American workers. Daddy is skilled.

- There are 120 houses for foreign-born people.

- 8 whole houses for doctors—doctors are men because women are not allowed to be doctors. They are lined up on a muddy hill. Missus Meadows says that this should be 26 houses, not 8—I do not understand this.

- 22 homes for men nurses and 48 for women nurses—I am not sure if this is right.

The new houses will be made of timber, and they will all get electric—a lot of timber for Daddy to haul. The houses come in parts by rail and get bolted together like a puzzle.

I wonder if my family would get a foreign-born house—we could not live in the bachelor houses because Daddy is not a bachelor for sure. I guess we are not allowed to live in the big houses because they are only for supervisors, chemical engineers, and the owners of the haberdashery and drug store.

Houses arrive in pieces that can be quickly assembled.

The skilled workers must all be Americans. I know Americans are very skilled. I am not sure where everybody else would fit in—like Mister Hart who takes care of our horses or the Melungeons who are very shy people who live in West Virginia, Virginia, and North Carolina. They are Indian and colored and white all at the same time, so I do not know where they will live. We should all get to choose where to live.

It would be very different from the farm if we lived in the big town—their houses have small gardens in the front yard for flowers and a space to grow vegetables out in the backyard. I wonder if the deer eat the flowers and the turtles eat the tomatoes like they do at our farmhouse.

We have all kinds of fun things now—a showboat and bucking broncos and rodeos and foot races. We have six new moving picture houses, and they might show *Tarzan of the Apes* there. It makes me wish I lived in the middle of the boomtown, and not on our farm. I think sometimes Mother feels the same way even if out loud she says the new boomtown is dirty and she would not want to live there ever! But after Mother goes to her World Club meetings I can tell she has new ideas in her head. She wants to be part of the modern future even if she says she loves things just like they are. I know I want a furnace and a telephone like the fancy houses.

***

Ann and Abigail could not wait to tell me all about the big city when they got home from Charleston. Last year we were just a village with only seventy-five people. We are bigger now, but not as big as Charleston. They have three office buildings over ten stories high and big stores that sell fine dry goods. The stores are called A.W. Cox and O.J. Morrison. Mother said she would like to see the woolen mills someday.

In Charleston there are also five excellent hotels, nine restaurants, fifteen lunch wagons, five or six hospitals, and around twenty-four school buildings! Charleston has problems just like Nitro.

Bucking broncos at a rodeo

Everyone who got to go to Charleston got to drink a Coca-Cola—very scarce on account of the war. Ann's daddy got everybody a tea-toast with frosting.

We saw all sorts of ready-to-wear dresses, and some had furbelows—Ann told me this.

They are here on my new dress—Abigail said this next. Her dress has a blue sash—the dress is made of white lawn material with cherries and blue flowers.

Abigail's mother got a new dress too, in a brand-new design—Abigail would not stop bragging about it. I looked at the furbelows on her dress and I think they are very easy to sew—just ruffles.

Even if Charleston is bigger and fancier, we have the same water running past us here in the Great Kanawha River.

Elise and Emmaline

April 23, 1918

Elise and Emmaline live in the mansion houses like Abigail and Ann. When they come around to play they pretend I am not there—just because they live on silk stocking row.

I do not see what this has to do with being friends. Their big mansions have a sunporch. At our farm we just go outside if we want sunshine!

I have always felt different but sometimes they ask me questions.

Does your farmhouse have a furnace Ana? They ask me. They know it does not.

Yesterday they told me my school dress looked almost as good as a store-bought. They were making a secret joke. I know my face turned hot and red and I tried to hide it—they saw.

When I told Mother about it I could tell it made her sad. Her advice was not any good. She said you must smile and walk away or break in and start talking about how much fun you have in the haybarn.

Now I wish I never told her about it because she will ask me every day if I am taking her advice.

The next time I send a *Victory Chronicle* I will sign it Ana, the only true war correspondent! How about that!

At least Ivy is now a fast friend too. She does not tell anyone the secrets I tell her—only one other friend. We must all try to get along.

There have been riots in other places and President Wilson is worried about people who do not want to work together. We all have to get along in this war emergency. I hope we all work together even after victory.

Here in Nitro it will give the President comfort to know we are mostly getting along together—except we have a white YMCA and a colored YMCA. This does not make sense—we all work together all day.

I have now learned about one real war profiteer—will tell Noble. I will also tell the Mayor and the police chief. Mister McCallister told us that Mister Fields is taking up rent—Mister McCallister says this is wrong because the houses are free—paid for by the United States of America. War profiteer!

Missus Patteson says her beds have bedbugs. This worries me—maybe workers only stay here for forty-three days because they cannot have a real house for their families and it is not nice with pests like lice and bedbugs.

City Girl

*A**pril 25, 1918*

I am a city girl now. Very modern!

Mother—if you are reading this—part of me will always be your country girl, but part of me is a city girl.

Today we were having fun skipping rope and singing a modern rhyme:

> Down in the valley where the green grass grows
>
> There sat Emmaline as sweet as a rose
>
> She sang, she sang, she sang so sweet
>
> Along came Tommy and kissed her on the cheek

Right then Noble came over and warned us city girls about war profiteering again! He probably just stole a licorice stick. It was all black around his lips and his nose.

Noble asked us to meet him as soon as possible at the Closet. Only a very few people know about the Closet. It is a big stand of proud pine trees growing close to each other in the woods right by school. It is a private place to talk. Even after the leaves on the other trees have fallen for winter, there are still deep dark shadows at the Closet. Huge wild grapevines grow there. They wind around the tree trunks and twist up to the very tops of the trees. Even the biggest trees finally get choked to death. The small branches die first and get caught up on the big branches when they fall and get stuck until the wind breaks them all apart. The vines are so strong we can swing on them.

I was thinking that we should never in a hundred years go meet Noble—but Ann and Abigail said they would meet him there immediately. I waited for them on the swing until everybody got there.

Noble struck a serious pose. He gave us a note and said I have written down three important war facts for you:

> Number one is just one word—MONEY.
> Number two is five words—PEOPLE ARE TALK-
> ING ABOUT YOU.
> Number three is—DO YOU KNOW WHAT
> MURDER IS.

I did not tell him that number three was a question not a fact, because he just ran away in the woods. We were afraid that number one meant he thought we were stealing money, because there is so much money moving around now—the United States of America is paying for everything—even new furniture. But about number two—people do talk about us and our amazing war work. We are war correspondents. People are counting on us.

Mother—if you are reading this—just happened in a dream. We did not meet up with Noble in the woods.

Industrial Nursing

A *pril 27, 1918*

On Saturdays, after my chores are done, I get to go to Ann's house or Ivy's house. One of my chores is to hang the wash on the clothesline with clothespins. Then I have to bring it back in the house at about four o'clock. This is annoying when the clothes are frozen solid in the winter.

Winter has all sorts of annoyances, like how we have to chop up the ice if the water buckets freeze over. Mabel eats lots of oats and hay in the winter. Winter is over now, so I finished my chores very quickly.

Advertisement for women workers in Nitro

Then I went to Ann's house and learned all about industrial nursing. I am excited about the new industrial nurse work. Missus Moody told us that it took a long time to develop the new field of industrial nursing.

When we finished nursing school, we had special training on hazards and health in factories. This is why we are called industrial nurses. There are even new laws for the new field—Missus Moody told us all of this.

Learning about it made me want to become an industrial nurse myself!

Ward nurse in uniform

Missus Moody says the nurses are working to bring something called industrial hygiene into the war factories—things like keeping children away from jobs, eliminating overwork and protecting against poisons. They also want to make sure that children have someone to care for them when their daddies and mommies go to work. They want to get rid of poverty and break down the taboo around telling where babies come from. I said we needed a code word if we were going to keep talking about this part. Ann called me silly.

These are all huge goals!

Navy nurses in uniform

Ann is very proud of her mother. She has a picture of navy nurses standing together in their uniforms. They have a uniform with a divided skirt for when they need to ride horseback. They cannot wear jewelry—only a watch. Missus Moody started out as a navy nurse in 1904. Now some nurses go to war in France. Ann has read *The Short History of Nursing*—not really a short book at all. In the book she said my mother could only be a mother-house nurse. I think she wanted to be mean.

There are more important jobs for women too. The Signal Corps telephone operators need people who can speak more than one language, like French. The operators are called the Hello Girls. They help the soldiers in the trenches so that they can send messages to the generals behind the battle lines.

Americans raised one hundred fifty million dollars for the American Red Cross. They train the nurses to help soldiers wounded in battle. Everyone pitched in to raise money—the YMCA, the Knights of Columbus, the Hebrew Association, and the Salvation Army.

Ann wanted us to make a list of the poison chemicals to avoid according to the industrial nurses:

- Sulfuric acid

- Nitric acid

- Mixed acid

- Sulfur dioxide

- Sulfur trioxide

- Caustic soda

- Nitrocellulose—our town name!

- Mixed dust

- Gas fumes

- Platinum—this is used to make platinum chloride. I saw a picture of the platinum when I went with Daddy to Sigmon's restaurant to eat a toasted-cheese sandwich. Mister

Withrow said they will need one million pounds of platinum, so there will be guards there all the time. Someone else said it is one million dollars of platinum, not pounds. Which is it?

Platinum with guards

There are all sorts of new things at Plant C—not just the industrial nurses. They can build with acid-proof brick now—safer. Missus Moody is proud of the new changing houses for men and women to wash the poisons off. There is a fumigation station and a house for removing lice—over one hundred treatments for acid burns at the hospital—good thing they built escape chutes in case of a terrible emergency.

Dear Mister President,

This *Victory Chronicle* is about our women workers. I am sure you know about the industrial nurses and the telephone operators and all the other women workers who are fighting hard for the war effort. Here in Nitro we might need as many as four thousand women workers.

Everyone here in Nitro is very grateful for your efforts to give us houses. We have learned how to build a whole street in just one day, so that tells you how well plans are coming along. But one problem with houses is about the women workers.

Missus John D. Rockefeller Junior has a committee for the Young Women's Christian Association. She has written a lot of things that are important for women workers:

1. A single room is more sanitary and moral.
2. A matron is needed for supervision, and she must be of the highest quality.
3. There must be at least one shower for every ten women—bathtubs are unsanitary.
4. The kitchen and dining room need a trained woman who can cook wholesome food. The women

should not choose their own food—in case they do not eat wholesome foods and get sick.

5. Women must have innocent recreation and a large room for visitors.

6. Foreign girls need an American woman to help them learn to speak English—my Daddy is Italian but I am not foreign so I do not need help with this.

7. Women should even own their own houses if they want to.

Missus Rockefeller has thought of EVERYTHING!

Signed,
Ana, Ann, and Abigail

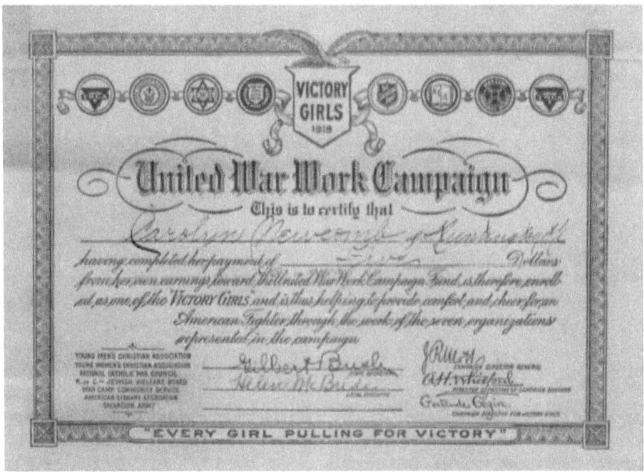

Victory Girls certificate from the United War Work Campaign. For enlarged image, see Appendix.

Questions for My
Fast Friends

*A**pril 28, 1918*

Today is Sunday—a day of rest, but I wish I could meet up with my fast friends! I have so much to ask them, so I need to write it all down. Writing about them is almost as good as seeing them. I hope I get to introduce them to President Wilson when this is all over.

Their streets have wooden sidewalks to keep out the mud—I already know they even have their very own telephone in their house. It is connected to telephone wires that are strung up on poles. The houses all share the telephone line—Ann can hear what other people are saying if she picks up the phone very quietly. She has number 309R.

I wish we had a telephone on the farm so that I could hear valuable information for the *Victory Chronicles*. I could call Noble's mother, who knows more than anybody else.

As fast as we write, Nitro grows faster. Plant C seems to stretch on forever and ever. We are not allowed to be anywhere near the laboratory buildings, and we know better than to go close to the ammunition testing grounds. There are walls shaped like pyramids—thick at the bottom for ammunition to go into when they fire off a test. We can see the walls when we play in the hills behind at the Devil's Tea Table—a big pile of rocks with one big flat rock and smaller rocks that look like chairs.

Ammunition loading laboratory

Here is my list of questions for the next time we meet up:

- Did we explain to the President why nitrocellulose is so important to make gunpowder in Nitro? Our name tells the whole world we are a modern scientific town doing important wartime work. Ann says that falling rain has something called nitric in it—hard to think about because it falls down on our fields too.

- Did we finish copying down all the names of the Explosives Plant C buildings? This is extremely necessary for producing smokeless powder in a hurry.

- We might need to tell how many more horses are needed. Mister Hart said maybe twenty thousand—sounds like too many to me. It will take a long time to get so many horses broken.

- We should make a list of the countries that workers are coming here from—like Italy!

- We must write to the President about farmers like Daddy who are worried that the time is coming soon when their oxen and horses will not be needed anymore.

- We must finish our list of dangerous chemicals!

- We need to know more about how we are meeting our safety needs. We now have eighteen watchtowers along with horse patrols and river patrols. What else?

Watchtower at Plant C

So many questions—we must not lose heart. We are the only ones who can do reporting because we live right here on the spot. Give us courage! Our *Victory Chronicles* are so important for President Wilson and for history.

Citizen Soldiers from Many Countries

May 1, 1918

There are so many Nitro citizens from countries all over the world who live here now—all soldiers for victory.

Ann's mother had hospital records at their house when I went there. We looked at them when her mother was not around. The hospital records were full of good news and bad news about all kinds of people I do not know.

1. Dorothy Weir recovered.

2. Oscar Ebert died. Noble says he was murdered because he knew about the crimes of the war profiteers. He says someone pushed him in front of an ammunition test on the testing grounds and he got blown up. His body is in the cadaver chamber.

3. Saran Fricke died.

4. Alice Stephens—nurse—died.

5. Lora Ruby improved.

6. Alex Christianson left the hospital to elope with his sweetheart. This is so dear to me.

7. Rod Martin—teamster—improved. What is a teamster?

8. Doctor Nutter recovered.

9. Peter Norban improved.

10. Luther Bateman—policeman—back at work.

11. Albert Moreno left the hospital against the doctor's advice.

12. Grace Rupert—chemist—cured.

13. John Constantino is well. I think he works around sulfuric acid. He lives right next to our farm and goes with Daddy to drink rhubarb wine every Saturday. They drink it out of a hose that comes out of the barrel.

Every single person who had anemia died, and also people with typhoid fever.

So sad to be a nurse!

It is important that we remember all of these people because they all are working for the same cause—victory! Some gave their lives for this cause.

Abigail looked at the records too.

Over two thousand people have been to the hospital for treatment she said. She did this with arithmetic. She multiplied forty-five records on each page by fifty-nine pages in the log.

She smiled at me but we argued about how many times I ask her to do the sums over for our *Victory Chronicles.*

I did ask Abigail to count up how many have died. She must do that.

Cadaver chamber

We also found a chart in the records of how many people can stay at the hospital:

- Section A barracks: 36 beds for detention of workers or soldiers who break the very strict rules. There are guards for this section.

- Children's ward: 32 beds.

- Isolation ward: 80 beds.

- Maternity ward: 20 beds.

- Double ward: 136 beds—it was marked down that the future double wards will only have 58 beds. Does this mean victory will come soon?

- Emergency hospital H: 26 beds.

- Private ward: 40 beds.

- Emergency dressing stations in sections F, L, and M: 10 stations for women and 28 stations for men. I think this is where people get fumigated to take away poison chemicals.

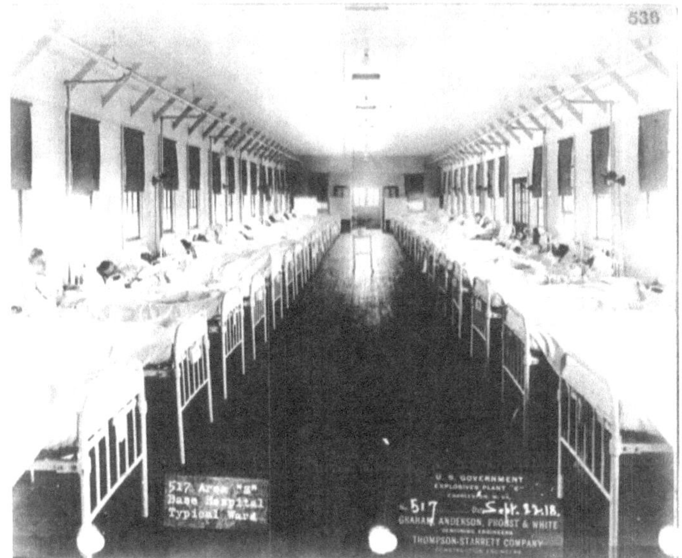

Hospital ward

This adds up to three hundred seventy beds, I think. Abigail will know. But the doctors told Missus Moody that they might have to build extra rooms to equal four hundred eighty beds. Not true. Noble said that when we showed him these numbers. There have been way more than four hundred acid burns already.

We live in dangerous times!

It is no wonder people are so worried—I worry all the time.

When Abigail's brother Owen was born her daddy took her to the ward but somebody told him that children are not allowed to visit the hospital. In the hospital there is sickness from nephritis, pneumonia, trench fever, Spanish flu, shell shock, acid burns, and more. Children should not be near that.

The World Club and Windtryst Farm

May 3, 1918

I am leery about this new modern club called the World Club. Not everybody gets to be a member. Mother and Ann's mother are very proud to be members, so maybe it is okay. We saw a picture of some of the members. Noble's mother was there too.

Ann is not afraid to ask questions—she asked her mother what they do in the World Club.

We want to help the world, help our daughters, and someday every woman! Missus Moody said this. She sounded very proud.

She said that the members will march in the victory parades when the time comes. Abigail thinks the club helps in the war effort and it could be about the problem of liquor or about women getting allowed to vote.

Many women are doing lots of things right now to be allowed to vote. They have chained themselves up to fences and held marches and strikes. Women get put in jail for things like that.

I am glad that I can walk across the railroad tracks over to Twenty-First Street and meet up at Ann's house to work on the *Victory Chronicles*. Ann lives in one of the houses for engineers—her sunporch has lots of glass windows. It is nice out there.

Today Ellen came along with me—she is not allowed to work with us! She might start to cry about everything I do—even my idea to make posters to tell everybody in Nitro to be sure to buy war bonds. So she has to play with Harry and his pet snake that he hides under his shirt just to scare us.

World Club meeting

Mother gets strange ideas in her head at World Club meetings. That is why I am not so sure about it. One day she came home from a meeting and told Daddy our farm should have a proper name.

She said we should be called Wyndtryst Farm because we live right where the winds meet.

Daddy smiled some, but he did not like that at all.

In our family we are Methodists. Methodists have very strict rules against bragging. We believe in modesty, and naming our farm a fancy name would be acting differently from our beliefs. But I know that we all do things that are different from the Methodist beliefs sometimes.

Mother and I are both are becoming jealous of the new modern ways like the furnaces in the fancy houses. Mother wants a furnace—I want a telephone. That is not like a good Methodist.

Ice Plant

May 10, 1918

I was at Abigail's house looking for more reports we might need to borrow for just one day for our *Chronicles*. I am supposed to come straight home after school—but Mother and Missus Palmer were at the World Club meeting again, and I think my sister Ellen is old enough to walk home by herself. I told her myself many times about being careful when she crosses the tracks.

The railroad tracks are right beside the ice plant where people get their ice blocks to keep things cold. The ice plant delivers ice to the milk factory, which makes four thousand gallons of milk every day. People can get ice blocks if they have iceboxes.

I know Ellen will tell on me at supper and pretend to cry because I made her walk home by herself. This is wartime! I am a war correspondent! I have important work to do!

The World's Biggest
Liar

*M**ay 12, 1918*

Noble thinks he scares us but he is just making me mad! Yesterday he came up to us when we were skipping rope and ordered us to let him look at the *Chronicles* before we send them in.

You must take information out of your reports—especially the numbers! He said this exactly, trying to be scary.

He just wishes he was a war correspondent! I cannot believe Harry thinks Noble is a hero to look up to.

I never let you look at the *Victory Chronicles* before, and I will not show you now either—I told him this. I know I sounded brave.

Noble's face was as red as the beets we pull out of the ground. BEET FACE!

You will be sorry if you put that out—he said this over and over.

We did not pay him any attention so he ran over to the end of the playground and picked up a big stick from the oak tree and waved it around over his head. Then he acted like he was going to stick it between Abigail's feet to make her trip up while she was skipping rope. It made us lose count—too bad because she was all the way up to forty-three jumps. We kept going even after we lost count. He will never get the best of us!

Kevin Hartman—the biggest bully in town—saw Noble right then. He hurried over and joined in. Someday soon I am going to sock him in the nose—could not right then because then all the boys would join in.

When I do sock him it will take him by total surprise!

Community shares time together at a soda fountain

Noble still had his beet face—he was yelling about secret incursions into the plant by people who come down the Kanawha River and steal things in the night. Harry joined in and pulled my dress sleeve so hard that I dropped my jump rope. We just started over with jump number one and did not pay them any attention.

They do not know what we know—I whispered this to Ann and Abigail after the boys finally went away. There are horse patrols—four hundred saddle horses for sure safety!

The boys had gone to talk to Elise and Emmaline. Those two will probably be moving picture stars with their pretty hats. The boys say they are dream girls. Then they call me dreaming girl just to be mean.

Elise and Emmaline are planning a big party. Noble is going. Maybe he is in love with both of them at the same time.

I saw Mabel watching a locomotive go across our pasture—she looked confused. The two centuries are happening at the same time more than ever—even the horses know. War plants have grown right out of our farms just like our crops. Workers are coming from all over the world to our boomtown. And we are working hard to be able to produce our share of five hundred thousand pounds of gunpowder every day for the war. This seems like a miracle to me. Farms—to factories—to victory!

I hope the new century brings a new way to water livestock in the wintertime. I hate chopping up the ice when the buckets freeze up—maybe there will be a new sewing machine for Mother so she will not need to push the treadle with her foot when she makes our dresses.

Mother if you are reading this—I promise I am not sick of our last century of life, and I will never stop riding.

In spite of those boys annoying us today we wrote a new letter to the President.

Dear Mister President,

In these dark times before victory I want to assure you of our efforts to bring us to a speedy win! It is important for you to know that our effort comes right from our hearts. Everywhere we go we see the progress that people are making—they are very happy to know we are telling you about it. They are so proud and they want to keep American spirits high! We are all soldiers for victory here in Nitro.

Children can buy the official Nitro picture postcards and send them out to you. They hope to have your autograph someday. Well—these other people can try to write to you about our progress here in Nitro but they are not war correspondents like us.

We are going to make posters to put in the window of the haberdashery store so that everybody will work even harder and buy more war bonds. We have lots of ideas about what to put on the posters:

HORSES AND TRAINS WILL WORK TO-
GETHER FOREVER!
OUR TREES GREW UP TO BE YOUR TRAIN
TRACKS!
JUST LIKE OUR OXEN—WE ALL PULL AS
ONE!
WE WILL GROW VICTORY RIGHT OUT OF
THE GROUND IN A HURRY!

Change is happening so fast that sometimes a whole street of houses can be built in one day. Mister Pat-teson told us that when he went home to his street, he got lost because the next street was already built while he was working. Ever since the first bungalow was ready on January fifth our boomtown has been growing fast.

You said in your speech we need force without stint. There is no stint here—that is for sure! It is hard beyond belief when our soldiers march off to war, but we are building for victory. We are fighting The Great War!

Signed,

Ana Ariano, Ann Moody, and Abigail Palmer

Streets such as this one could be built in one day.

Major Mudd

May 20, 1918

Major Seeley W. Mudd was let go last week. He was one of the top engineers—the boss of the assistant directors—he had a lot of power and knowledge. He was the supervisor of the water supply, railroad systems, road systems, materials testing, control, and general construction.

Maybe he was a spy for the Germans and that is why he was let go. It is true that there are spies here working for Germany. We read about spies in *The Delineator*. Noble talks about them all the time. A woman named Louise Olivereau is in prison for ten years for interference with the draft. David Lamar had to go to prison for making secret plans against the United States of America—including hurting munition plants. That means all of us here in our boomtown. Thank goodness he is in New York—not nearby Plant C!

Maybe if we do an investigation we can find out what happened to Major Mudd. He lives in a house on Twenty-First Street where all the important leaders live. I do not know too much about them—his wife, Missus Mudd, is very shy. Right behind their house you can see the woods. If you go into the woods and climb up to Devil's Tea Table, you can see the roof of their house.

Very important.

***

I am writing again—we just got back from our investigation. We started with a walk down Twenty-First Street. We went between their house and the one next to it for clues. If anybody asked us—we were going to say we were looking for walnuts. I told Ann and Abigail it is not walnut time yet—they said it does not matter. I promised to write all this down.

- No victory garden in the backyard—very important to the war effort!

- No flower garden in the front.

- Missus Mudd does not go to World Club meetings.

- Their boy Larry is very shy.

- Mister and Missus Mudd never come to the new things in Nitro—not even the famous foot races.

We will keep our eyes and ears open for sure.

There is even more exciting news! We are invited to come to the police station on Saturday to meet Mister Daniels—the Mayor of Nitro. Saturday is not very good for me because it is a chore day—I have to shovel manure out of the run-ins. But I will figure out a way to get there. It will take some planning but I promise I will be there. We must be getting honors for being war correspondents. I will not even tell my friends about my chores so that they do not doubt that I will be going to the police station. Maybe I can ask John or Sarah or Ellen to take my turn on my chores. I could share my books with them.

Foot race

Little Bit of Truth Interview

*M*ay 25, 1918

We were the first to get to the police station this morning—Mayor Daniels gave us chairs to sit on. We were in his own office—he was behind his very important desk!

We remembered our manners and said we are pleased to meet you Mayor Daniels Sir.

I was right—the meeting was all about our *Victory Chronicles*. We are more famous than we ever knew! He gave us some information to help us write our next *Chronicle*. I copied lots of things down:

- There are 115 patrolmen and a police chief. The patrolmen find any breaking of rules and regulations. They will also guard our new Day and Night Bank.

- A new secret intelligence service will be put together soon.

- We have 380 Indian guards from every state with excellent training.

- He showed us a shiny picture of all the officers wearing their uniforms looking very important. He said it was very important to let everybody know how hard the policemen work.

- He showed us the jail cells—seven for men and three for women.

- He asked us if we know anybody who works in the boxhouse or in the chronograph house. Ann knows Mister Cerullo because he came to her house two times to get for information. We know Mister Raines—puts the ammunition boxes together—and Noble's daddy of course.

- He asked us how many *Victory Chronicles* we have already mailed out to President Wilson. We did not know for sure the answer—I got a red tomato face.

- He said we are doing important work and should bring information directly to him first and not to tell any of it to anybody—sometimes there might be things in our *Chronicles* that are important for the police to know—keep an eye out for criminals.

- He asked us if we are careful with arithmetic—YES—I am very afraid Abigail might have made some mistakes—maybe we are not so good at arithmetic. I will ask her again to double check all of our sums—this will make her mad.

- He wanted to know if we get information from our daddies—I said lots of it. Abigail said a lot of it is top secret. Brave!

When we went out of his office he told us one of the policemen would check up on us every now and then. He did not wait for us to answer—we would never share any secret information we find with anybody but him and the police—we already know exactly how many brave policemen and guards we have.

Indians were crucial participants in West Virginia's war effort.

You Big Dummies!

May 27, 1918

I do not know how Noble found out about our meeting with the Mayor, but he sure had a lot to say about it!

You big dummies he yelled out—the police only want your *Victory Chronicles* to find out what you know and what you send out—you lost a lot—they do not think you are doing important work—that meeting was not an honor at all!

Somehow he hooked this up to the war profiteering he always goes on about.

Study your own facts—you should know by now that war profiteering is a crime. These criminals will kill you just to keep their secret money if you find out too much—they want to steal the platinum—one million dollars—he told us we could be burned up in acid vats or crushed in the coal crusher! You better stop now before it is too late he said and then he called us dunces! That is when he turned to being just plain cruel.

You are all peas—smaller than the peas in your garden! Rum runners, rum runners, you better run!

Harry joined in because he is always on Noble's side

Ann has a potato face—you are double triple dummies! Harry yelled out.

Elise and Emmaline both keep their eyes open and their mouths shut—they listen to my warnings. That is how dream girls act! Noble went on and on taunting us.

I am so mad at Noble—I am ready to sock him.

We ran away—right into Andrew and Kevin telling Ellen that Mister Ebert was in the morgue after he got murdered for knowing too much about war profiteering—people who know too much get burned up in acid or get crushed in the crusher is what they told her. Well, if that is true his body would not be in the cadaver room. Take that Noble!

When Ellen gets scared she bites her fingernails—she sure was biting them right then. Those boys just want to see her cry. I would like to sock them too!

Something Horrible

May 28, 1918

Something horrible just happened. Ann's mother was very mad when she got home from the World Club meeting to-day—she came back from the meeting early when I was still at Ann's house.

She said she could not even call the meeting to order because everyone was talking over each other. They were talking loud on purpose to make sure she would hear everything they said. They wanted her to get angry.

She pointed at Ann—and do you know what they were talking about? They were talking about you!

Missus Dudding said we told everybody the letter she had from President Wilson to his little friend was not real. Missus Zeins said we made fun of her collections. Missus Beckley said we were the rudest and most impudent girls she had met in her life. Missus Lanier said Mister Lanier told her I spit in his boots and his lunch pail—a big LIE. Somebody blamed us for causing Mister Mudd to be let go because we told everyone he is a spy—and we spread the rumor about typhoid fever. Somebody told Missus Moody that the Mayor called us in because we are in trouble.

Ann tried to explain that none of this is true—I do not know if Missus Moody believed us. She frowned at us and told us that truthful words stand the test of time but lies are soon exposed. I guess that means she will wait before she makes up her mind about us. Ann fell to pieces and cried and cried. I went home right then.

All our facts about the real letter are true—the reports we read are all put in on a new invention called a typewriter. I did not spread rumors about typhoid fever!

Butterick Patterns

June 6, 1918

The United States Secretary of War Mister Newton Baker is coming to Nitro!

He wants to see all the progress we made to help out with our gunpowder goals. I just know he will be pleased. We went from a little village to a very big boomtown in just one half of one year!

I think lots of important people will meet up with him like Mister Mohler who owns the sawmill and the pencil factory and Mister Payne who has a lot of land.

What good news! It almost makes me forget about the spies and the rumors that we meddle in the war effort.

Maybe the showboat will be here when Mister Baker comes. Sometimes we got to see a showboat called the Stanley—named after Doctor Stanley Livingston—explorer! That ship sank so now the Greene Line sends the Greenland showboat down the river to us.

I wish President Wilson was coming to visit—we will write all about it in our next *Victory Chronicle* so that he will not miss one thing. This will be a very important visit!

Noble hopes we get a chance to tell Mister Baker our worries about war profiteers. Maybe we should write it in a letter. I am starting to think Noble is right. It makes me very scared, but I believe in us! Mister

Baker might think we are only silly little girls—but we are working hard to tell everybody to be on the lookout for criminals.

Mother says we must all have new pretty dresses for the celebration. She let us pick out a dress pattern like the ones the Butterick Pattern Company has on tissue paper. I saw the pictures in *The Delineator*.

Showboat

We went to the Lock Seven dry goods store to look at the patterns for Sarah, Ellen, and me. I liked a pattern numbered 2511 by McCall's, which is a suit called a street costume. I would like to make it in navy blue percale! And I would like to pair it up with pattern 7061 by Butterick—a beautiful hat tied up in the front and tied with a ribbon under my chin. Mother is thinking of peplums for herself—she looked at patterns for women while I looked at little girl patterns for Ellen and Sarah. There are patterns for stout women too.

Ann has ready-to-wear dresses, so her mother does not need to sew a new dress for her. We saw lovely ready-to-wear dresses at the store—cost a whole $2.95 and all the way up to $15.95 if you want furbelows.

There were also bassieres covered up with tissue paper. I just might want a brassiere someday.

Mother almost never tells my brother John Dominique he cannot have pocket money to play at the pool hall but she will not let me buy a brassiere ever—even if they are for sale at the Lock Seven dry goods store.

I do feel very sorry for John because he wants to fight for our country—he cannot because his leg is all twisted. He helps out a lot at our farm—very important in wartime.

Drugstore and haberdashery at Plant C. This became the site of the former Nitro World War I Memorial Museum.

I am remembering a story I read called "Jimmie the Sixth Who Came of a Long Line of Distinguished Lawyers but Preferred to be

a Law Unto Himself." Mother's contribution to the war emergency
made me think of it because Jimmie wanted to be a costume designer.
He did not want to go out by the day, either. He wanted his own shop
in New York City. In the story a woman named Louise asked him if
he would have a bag full of patterns and bon-tons and a bag of scissors
around his waist. She asked him how he could talk with a mouth full of
straight pins. She was not a nice person. The story had a happy ending,
though. Jimmie sold dresses for a lot of money in important cities and
his victory garden recipes became famous also. Louise had to spend
her time doing church work because she never became rich.

I will never forget about Jimmie and Louise. My very own mother
could be like Jimmie because she can sew almost everything. She could
put her money into the new Nitro Day and Night Bank. Someday I
will have to think about all the recipes we made from dandelions and
goldenrod. Yuck! Not today.

Noble's Teasing

June 14, 1918

I take back what I said about listening to Noble! He just enjoys torturing us.

Today he tried to hand me a diagram. It was probably the instructions for making ammunition boxes because Noble's daddy cuts the wood and nails up the boxes at the boxhouse. Noble thinks it should go in the next *Victory Chronicle*.

But as soon as he held it out—Elise tried to grab it and I grabbed at it too. Noble saw we both wanted it—he waved it over his head so neither of us could grab it and he walked away! I chased right after him and got a look at the diagram—he is the dunce.

If we get kidnapped and shipped off in ammunition boxes—I hope we get sent to France. We will learn French and go England and Brave Little Belgium on the way home.

Mister Newton Baker, Secretary of War

June 18, 1918

Ann confided to Abigail and me that she had a horrible nightmare about a big disaster.

There was a loud noise—then she saw a giant explosion at the plant that made a huge green cloud that hung over the whole town before floating to the ground. The whole sky over Nitro was bright green!

She wiped her eyes right then.

A rider on horseback galloped down Twenty-First Street calling out for everybody to hide somewhere safe. He was already covered in green dust like springtime pollen. The cloud burned her eyes and she could not find Harry to take him to the basement. She could not even call out for him because her throat was frozen like ice. Her mother was at the hospital—right there on the spot in the middle of the explosion.

How terrible for Ann! She must have felt awful when she woke up—at least she realized it was just a dream.

We all have dreams like that—lots of people are worried about poison in the air.

Mister Muck dug a tunnel right under his house. His tunnel leads deep into the woods. He is a coal miner for Elk River or Blue Creek

Coal, so this must be how he could dig such a long tunnel without his house falling on top of it.

The tunnel must let out somewhere near Devil's Tea Table or maybe in the woods past Third Avenue. We will go explore—Harry is not allowed to come with us. I keep telling him this but he keeps on coming anyways—saying the whole time that he has his pet snake Bart hidden under his shirttail. One time he rustled some weeds and said there was a tiger behind the tree. Ann smacked him on his head and he cried—such a bother.

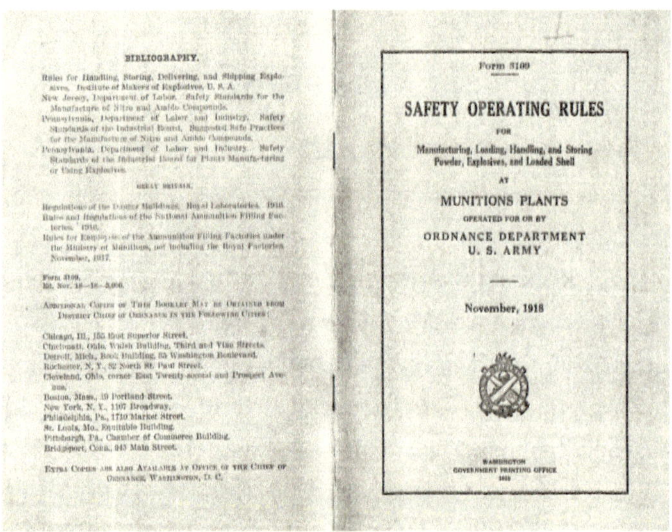

Pamphlet of safety rules for munitions plants

We have all agreed that we should write a *Victory Chronicle* for Secretary of War Mister Newton Baker before he comes to Nitro. His big visit will be on July 11, only twenty-three days away. He will inspect the plant and go in because all United States government officials can go inside. Our *Victory Chronicle* letter will make sure that Mister Baker knows to check that the safety rules for making gunpowder are being carefully followed. This is VERY important—we are glad he is coming to check! Maybe Ann will start to feel better about her dream.

Dear United States Secretary of War Mister Newton Baker,

We are writing to you from Nitro, West Virginia, where you will visit us soon to inspect our ammunitions plant, Plant C. We have concerns about safety booklets number 1888 and 309, which we have from Ann's house. Every worker has a copy of the manuals—they were made in 1912 and 1914 by the United States Government Printing Office.

Our concern is that it is very important that these rules are followed by everybody at the plant and the managers and doctors. We hope that you will come inspect the plant and make absolutely sure that the rules are being followed.

We have picked out the most important rules for you to check on:

1. Workers need to read their manuals to understand the dangers of the toxic materials in the plant.
2. Nobody can use intoxicating liquors while they work—or eat lunch around the buildings.
3. Nobody can use matches or oil lanterns except in dire emergencies. Storekeepers must only sell safe-

ty matches, and there will be absolutely no smoking cigarettes inside the plant. Only hot water or steam should be used for heat. This is so important to avoid fire. They say some workers have a chew of tobacco—breaking the rules!

4. Hazardous materials must be removed from any buildings needing repairs before repairs begin. They must be wheeled out—not dragged. That is why they come into the plant on flat cars.

5. Cleanliness and orderliness must be the top concerns for everyone working around gunpowder.

6. There must be drowning tanks to drown anything in an acid state.

7. Only army and navy officers can carry weapons.

8. All entrances must be well lit and guarded at all times. Everyone must have a pass with their own name on it to enter.

9. Escape chutes are better for evacuation than stairs.

10. Smokeless powder must never be damp, since this would make weak gunpowder. But even the bad powder must be carefully packed in two paper bags to protect it from lime.

11. Special caution must be taken with picric acid. It cannot touch metal, and it will explode if it gets too hot!

We thank you from the bottom of our hearts for double-checking the safety at our plant. We are not allowed near the gunpowder testing grounds or the laboratory buildings to check for ourselves that everybody is following all the rules. Thank you for coming to Nitro. You will be very proud of all the work we are doing!

Signed,
Ana Ariano, Ann Moody, and Abigail Palmer

P.S. Do not worry about making sure that we are digging coal. We know how to do that here in West Virginia!

Escape chutes

Mister Baker Arrives Soon

June 26, 1918

When I told Mother that Abigail and I were invited to Ann's house for supper on July 10th—the night before Mister Newton Baker gets to Nitro—she said we must be very mindful of our manners. We do not know many manners at our table. John wipes his mouth with his shirttail. Sarah and Ellen and I have had lessons on manners from Mother—but we do not have a butter knife or a dessert spoon like they have at fancy dinners. We only get one fork and one spoon, and sometimes a knife if we are eating chicken.

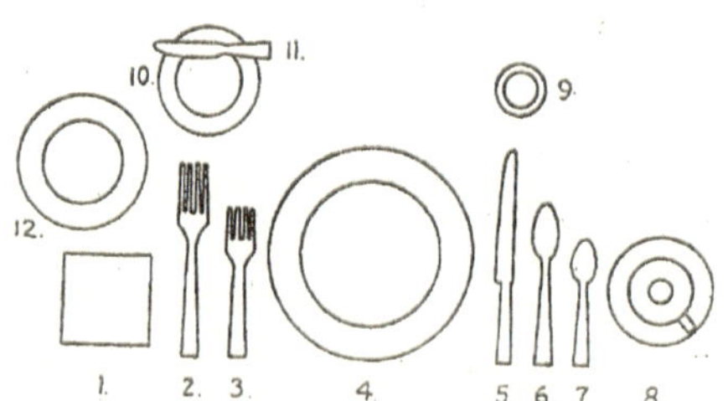

1. Napkin. 2. Fork. 3. Salad Fork. 4. Plate. 5. Knife. 6. Dessert Spoon. 7. Teaspoon. 8. Cup and Saucer. 9. Glass. 10. Bread and Butter Plate. 11. Butter Knife. 12. Salad Plate.

Diagram showing proper table setting

To teach us manners Mother cut out another picture from one of her magazines. It is named *All Around the Table*. It shows the right way to set up a table. We practiced with forks and spoons and acted like we had napkins. We were all well-behaved—no temper tantrums. But when Mother was not looking I pulled my skirt up over my drawers to make Sarah and Ellen laugh. John did not have to join in the lesson about manners with us.

Manners would even be more important if President Wilson was coming to Nitro for a grand banquet to celebrate victory.

Mother thinks she understands the new ways—maybe thinks she can see the future. That must be why she is planning out the whole summer for me. She is reading "Guide for the Junior Miss" and "Bandbox Look." These teach all kinds of new chores for girls. I have to iron my hair ribbons and wash my hairbrush and comb every Saturday night.

I am glad I am still invited to dinner even if I had a big argument with my friends again. I wanted to send Mister Baker all the steps for making smokeless powder but all in the right order. I told them we needed to look at all of the steps together. Abigail got very cross.

You always think you are the boss of us—but you are not! You probably do not even know how to put your own schoolwork in order—Abigail said to me just like that!

I did not cry even though Ann did not stand up for me even a little bit.

Then they both started talking about the beautiful hats and dresses they would wear when the Secretary of War Mister Baker comes to town. I did not say I will not have a hat to wear because Mother ran out of time to sew it. I will only have a bow ribbon in my hair. My heart is broken! I should have told them that my dress will last much longer than theirs—Mother is an excellent seamstress. They should be thankful for all the beautiful dresses Mother has sewn for the grownups in Nitro to wear for parties. Without a proper hat Ann and Abgail will look down on me.

It is hard not to be jealous. It is hard not to compare things when I am at Ann or Abigail's house on silk stocking row. The timbers for the floor are so shiny I can just about see myself in them. They get a new varnish every spring. They have a pantry for food instead of a cellar and a smokehouse like we have. They have electric lights hanging down from the ceiling and beautiful covers to scatter the light all through the whole room—brighter than lamps or candles—sidewalks and Tarvia on the streets—easy to walk on.

But I am NOT jealous! I love the farm—I do.

I copied down the steps from Mister Palmer's desk to show to Mister Baker. That way he can report right back to the President all about Nitro. I had to borrow the train map too for good measure—Abigail would not.

Mister Baker's Visit

July 2, 1918

I hope there will be a large parade when Mister Baker comes to Nitro next week. The soldiers can join the parade on horseback, and we will hang flags all along the streets. The whole parade could go down Twenty First Street. That way we can all stand on the wooden sidewalks. There should be a band playing trombones and saxophones and a car for every department of Plant C. The nurses and the Red Cross can march in their white uniforms—white aprons, white hats, white nylons, and white shoes. How impressive they will look!

I must tell the police chief right away about my idea! I hope Ann and Abigail will help me make up a slogan to put on a big sign for every department. For the Inventory Department, we could write: You get it—We count it! The brand-new auditorium will have more than six hundred seats, so maybe we can work in there. Mister Baker will watch the parade go by before he goes to see the mill. He will be so proud of us.

I hope with all my heart the pattern I picked out will make a beautiful dress for me to wear. I am trying so hard not to be jealous of Ann and Abigail's ready-to-wear dresses. Mother can tell how I feel, and she tries to cheer me up by talking about different materials—like colorful calico—or the new designs—like how dresses now end six inches above the floor. NO CALICO.

Gravy Boat

July 10, 1918

It is very late at night. Tonight was the night we ate supper with Ann's family. The whole night I was shy. I am glad I learned manners but there were still things I did not know. There was a gravy boat on the table that looked like it was pasted on a plate so the gravy could not spill over. I told them Mother does not let me eat gravy so they would not send the gravy boat around to me—I did not know what to do. We had a butter knife and a dessert spoon for the Jiffy-Jel. At home we just use a regular spoon for dessert.

I felt better when Abigail said we should go out on the sidewalk and jump rope.

> Down in the valley where the green grass grows,
> There sat Elise as sweet as a rose.
> She sang, she sang, she sang so sweet,
> Along came Bucky and kissed her on the cheek.

We sang another one—Abigail and Noble sitting in a tree. K-I-S-S-I-N-G.

Sometimes our nice dresses get tangled up in the jump rope—I can do fifty-two straight jumps.

Mister Woods passed by us with his trumpet—maybe to practice before the parade. There will be a parade just like I hoped, and I told the Mayor to hang up flags on all the poles.

Then Ann took my hand and squeezed my fingers.

Abigail and I will be up on the stage with Mister Baker tomorrow, and Elise and Emmaline too she said.

I already knew that her uncle D.C. would be on stage because he is very important. I guess they will all get to stand up there with their daddies—but not me. I tried to look delighted.

When I got home it was already dark—I could not get a word out about the supper. Even John did not tease me because he could see that my delight was not real. Mother tried to cheer me up—she told me that she put the hem in my dress for tomorrow, and that I will look beautiful. That only made me feel worse because it reminded me that I will not be up on stage in my new dress, and it made me remember I will not have the hat I wanted—Mother did not have time to sew it from the new pattern.

I kissed Mother and Daddy and went straight to bed right then.

I did not want to stay and let it slip out that tomorrow will not be the most perfect day. I had to tell somebody so I told Sarah about Ann and Abigail standing up on the stage and begged her not to tell. I do not want Mother to ever think I am jealous. Sarah did not understand—she just knew I was very sad. She said all the dirty words she knows.

Hell! Hell! Go to Hell! Horse Poo Horse Poo thrown at you!

I never cried even one tear. Hooray for me. I will try to be very happy tomorrow in spite of my misery. I always know the *Victory Chronicles* are important to President Wilson.

Baker's Day

July 11, 1918

I must pray after Mister Baker's visit—I know I have been prideful and envious because I have been coveting things and thinking about how Ann and Abigail have things I do not have. This is a sin. I feel very bad about it. I have been very selfish and only worrying about my dress.

We are getting dressed now because chores are done—I see that we will all look very nice—I should not have been so prideful. I think the streak of lightning that I saw for a second made me open my eyes to my own sins. Now I will work very hard to be better.

Mother made tatting that looks like lace on the collars of Ellen's and Sarah's calico dresses. Mother's dress is a very old black one but she used her clever tricks and skill at sewing to make it look brand new. She even used the new snap-on fasteners to snap on the collar of her dress. She changed her skirt and added a lot of blue material around her waist—way too much. She put new pockets on her skirt. She is beautiful—I saw the material she used for pockets when I was looking through her scrap bag to sew a dress for my doll Marian. I know she wanted a new dress made from serge material—I hope she loves her dress all the same.

Daddy will just wear his overalls—he is proud, but not in the sinful way. He is just proud that he is a worker in the war effort!

I was afraid I would have to wear a calico dress like Ellen and Sarah, but Mother made me a wonderful street dress that is the prettiest of all. It is made from dark blue broadcloth with a real lace collar that comes to a point under my chin. The skirt has full plaits with a wide white ribbon. Mother says a dropped waist design is the newest fashion. I know she worked very hard to sew our dresses—she has to keep pushing the treadle with her feet to make her machine go.

This is why tonight I will pray and ask forgiveness for being so prideful and greedy. From this day forward I must work hard to be more virtuous. I will not ever make fun of Reverend Fisher's rabbit eye again and I will forgive all of Noble's nasty lies. I will ask forgiveness for borrowing all the drawings and maps and the pictures I needed. I will pray every day.

I remembered just now that I never told my friends about the time I asked Noble which one of us was the prettiest.

None of you! You are all dunces and dummies he said.

Ann and Abigail would have their feelings hurt—it is a good thing they were not around.

I wonder if Ann and Abigail pray and ask forgiveness for their sins like the Methodists do. Elise is a Baptist—Emmaline says she is a Protestant. I told them I was a Christian!

Mother reminded me not to be a crosspatch just because I am not going to stand on the stage with Mister Newton Baker, even if Ann and Abigail get to. I want to ask him if he had time to read our letter, and if he feels right at home in Nitro because he is from Martinsburg, West Virginia. I hope Ann and Abigail remember to ask him. Maybe I can rustle my skirt so that they notice me—then I will tell them.

I have been cheerful for all twelve years of my life so I hope Mother knows I will not stop now. All that is left to do is put a bow in my hair, and then I will be ready to go. I feel very bad because I was upset my hat was not ready. I was being greedy and selfish. My ribbon will be pretty. My dress is almost like Abigail's and Ann's ready-to-wear dresses.

And your dress was made with love—that's what Mother told me.

This makes me feel more guilty about envy. I must pray.

Woman's Home Companion says to wear a stole for the evening. We do not have any stoles because all our animals are still alive! Another one of my jokes.

I hope and hope that Mister Baker has read our letter so that he knows what to look out for at Plant C. That is why I wish I was up on the stage with him—so I could tell him—not because I am envious.

This is called an adventure! I will start the next *Victory Chronicle* with these words:

Dear Mister President Sir,

We are so grateful our own Secretary of War came here
to Nitro so that he could tell you about all of the work
we are doing here. I hope this helps you rest easier. We
all gave him a big welcome!

When we got to the parade I saw that the American flags had been hooked onto the poles on Twenty-First Street exactly like I told the police chief and the Mayor to do. But it was not all smooth and perfect.

Do they still live in tents in Ariano? Charlie Mullins yelled out when he saw Daddy coming up the street.

I knew right then that trouble was ahead. I hoped he was just excited about our big day and making a joke—so I laughed very loud—that way Daddy would think it was a joke too. Like when the men call a man Hatrack because he does not work very hard or when they call

Mister Carter Grain Man because he drinks liquor. Hatrack and Grain Man always laugh and do not mind. Men are always calling out funny things out to each other. I was afraid Daddy might get mad and take all of us home.

I cannot even write what Daddy said back. Oh boy! He said a word that started with a D.

D.C. Jackling and Newton Baker, United States Secretary of War

Then the grand parade began, and the band marched down the street playing a patriotic song for Mister Baker. The wooden sidewalks were full of people cheering and clapping. The soldiers and nurses marched by in their uniforms. Mister Baker watched the whole parade. He cannot stay here very long because our hotel will not be ready until August.

I hope he still had plenty of time to check on Plant C!

The auditorium can hold six hundred people—I saw lots of men and women who do not even live here in Nitro but came to celebrate our big day. The women wore street dresses with satin and lace collars. I was a little worried about all these fancy people. This might be why Mother wants to name our farm Windtryst Farm.

Postcard showing the Nitro Hotel

It is so late, and it was a long day, I am getting very sleepy. But I must write down everything so that I can remember this day forever. I hope Mister Baker tells our President Wilson that he saw all of us living in two centuries at the same time. It is truly amazing!

The last thing I will write down today is my own prayer for tomorrow.

Dear Mathew, Mark, Luke, and John,
My cheeks do not need rouging,
My dress does not need lace,

My legs will never be silken,
Oh please fill Mother with grace.
Amen

I might send in my own prayer for the contest!

What a long and precious day! If I die before I wake, I pray the Lord my soul to take.

Early Victory Party for Newton Baker

July 12, 1918

There will be a grand costume party at Ann's house tonight to thank Mister Baker for his visit to Nitro.

I am going but Mother and Daddy do not get to go. I bet this is because they are afraid that Mother would sew the best dress-up costume for the party for herself and make everybody else look silly! Or maybe they thought Daddy would bring one of our oxen to the party—this is very funny! I guess that means not everybody gets to go. John says he does not care about parties but Sarah and Ellen looked a little bit sad.

Noble's parents will not be there either even if Noble's daddy is the mechanic foreman and a carpenter in the boxhouse—he is important to Plant C. I wish they got to go even if I hate Noble.

Elise and Emmaline will be there of course. They will both be fairies. They can flit around and hear things. That is a good way to get more important facts for our *Victory Chronicles*!

Mister Moody will dress like a jester—Abigail will be a circus clown. Missus Moody will be a royal queen.

I bet they will have a whole barrel of rhubarb wine, and maybe even cocktails!

I will walk right up to Mister Baker and ask him if he read the important safety manual we sent out to him. I already know some people break one safety rule—they have a chew of tobacco at the plant.

Did the safety look good at Plant C? I will say. Are we making fast progress? I hope you saw that we are very close to making our share of five hundred thousand pounds of powder every day for the war. It looks exactly like that in the reports. We copy it all down the way they do.

Elise and Emmaline in fairy costumes

Maybe Mister Baker will be impressed by my chemistry knowledge.

Ann's daddy teaches us about chemistry too. Almost every time we go to their house he tells us kids—N-a-C-l is awfully good on a tomato! That is just salt. Or he asks are you kids drinking plenty of H-2-O? This is just water!

Ann gets so annoyed and says his jokes are just plain not funny.

I hope I have enough time to say to Mister Baker thank you for giving us this project and also the rodeo, the showboat, the boxing arena, the bowling alley, and the two YMCAs. And I will ask him to thank Missus John D. Rockefeller Junior for the women's houses.

There is so much more I could say—like how Mother sewed my beautiful gypsy costume for the party and how the nurses are worried about typhoid fever. Maybe we should tell him about the rumors of war profiteering and murder! He is a very important man—maybe he could help us.

Be bold Ana!

Dear Mister President Wilson,

We went to a dress-up party last night for Mister Newton Baker to thank him for his visit to us here in Nitro. I heard him tell his great satisfaction with our progress. He even said that we are an inspiration to all of America! He is so happy that we are so close to being able to make our share of smokeless powder every day.

I hoped to meet him to tell him that we appreciate his inspection at Plant C—we did not get to speak to him.

Somebody at the party called us a camp. I do not know what he meant. If we are a camp—then we will not break camp until we win the Great War!

Signed by Real War Correspondents,
Ana, Ann, and Abigail

Mister and Missus Palmer did not show Abigail around to everybody tonight, so she did not act prissy. She had a glowing smile because it was painted on her face for her circus clown costume! Her eyebrow got smeared off.

Meany starts with M-E. I need to be a better friend! I will pray again tonight.

Women in costumes

We heard everything that Mister Baker said and all the people at the party. The chemists were talking about Mister Baker's regulations for the care and testing of smokeless powder materials. Moisture and very high temperatures can ruin the gunpowder, so they must be very careful when storing it. The men were talking about nitrocellulose and acid and alcohol. We heard the number four million pounds of gunpowder. So much!

The people at the party were still very sad about the Lusitania, which got sunk by German submarines. They hoped we will find a way to stop those evil submarines, especially since the Germans said they would stop sinking ships—but they kept right on doing it anyway!

Mister Hiss said that women dilute the workforce. Missus Moody told Mister Baker she knew he said it at an important meeting. She told him she found that notion absolutely ridiculous!

Missus Moody is so brave.

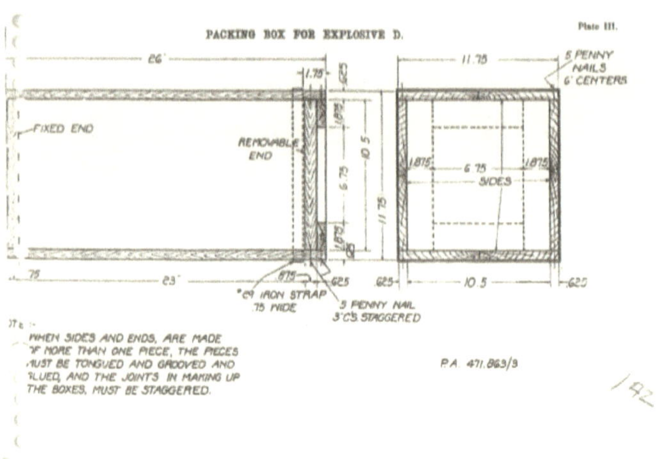

Plan for packing box

I saw the drawing of the important boxes we are making for packing and shipping the powder. Everybody was crowded around the table to get a look. The box has glue and wood and is put together so that only one end of the box can open. It is locked with iron straps. I wish Mister Carter had been there—he is the one who knows the most about the boxes.

The adults all drank cocktails, and Abigail made pictures of the grand party.

Cotton is poison—Abigail said this right out of the blue.

Not true! Mother sews cotton all the time—they use it at the plant too.

Abigail and I have more differences every day!

None of us was bold enough to say even one thing to Mister Baker—even though we made a list of things to tell him about. We missed our last chance. There are so many things he needs to know!

1. We are worried that Mister Raines might be a war profiteer. We wanted to come right out and say this to Mister Baker!

2. We wanted to ask if we are in danger—maybe this would have been silly. We are worried that we will be murdered by the war profiteers but we do not want to sound like little girls.

3. Missus Carter is a telephone operator and hears about war profiteering on the party line. We wanted to ask Mister Baker about this but the whole thing is too confusing to explain.

4. Mister Oscar Ebert could have been murdered by somebody who broke safety manual Rule 11—he got drowned in an acid tank or burned up. We saw the hospital records from Missus Moody.

In the end I was afraid to speak at all.

Atonement

July 27, 1918

We had a big poster sale to raise money for the war. But I had an evil thought—I need ten dollars of this money to buy Christmas gifts for my family. I will have to pray a lot to atone for this as Christmas draws near. I pray to the Father, Son, and Holy Ghost for forgiveness. I want my family to have gifts like Jesus Christ got on his birthday.

I hope I do not get sent down to hell for this—I will get a chance to make it up—put back the ten dollars when I join the pin-money club for girls who want to make money.

Mother will be very pleased with 3-in-one oil for her sewing machine, so that she does not have to push so hard on the treadle. I am not sure how much 3-in-one oil costs—maybe they will send me a sample for her to try. Then she could sew herself a new corset right away.

For Daddy I am dreaming of a fine pair of slippers.

For Ellen I can buy three Nitro postcards for her to send to her pretend friend—Ruby Lips.

For John a roll of plaster tape for sore feet.

And for Sarah a bottle of something that smells very nice.

I am remembering my prayer from a few weeks ago not to be greedy. I have to live up to this prayer.

Reading the Victory Chronicles

August 1, 1918

We know for sure that President Wilson is reading our *Victory Chronicles* to help him plan out the rest of the war. He said again that nobody will be permitted to make a fortune out of the war. This is pure proof that he is listening to us!

We are all so proud of our work. I believe we should send out every one of the pictures we borrowed to show it. I am afraid we might have lost some of them.

Then it will be our sacred duty to catch all the criminals and tie them up. We all agree that the ammunition boxes would be a good place for a criminal to hide extra things and steal them later. We looked at the box plans again at the victory party—some of them are still at Ann's house.

After we study the boxes again we will watch Mister Cooley and Mister Raines and Mister Cunningham to see if any of them are criminals. Each one of us will follow one of them—I want to follow Mister Raines. He is a top citizen, and his job is to lock up the boxes with iron straps when they are full of powder. That means he could sneak something in the boxes! I must ask him a lot of questions to make sure he is following the box instructions and not making any changes.

Mister Raines does not have a family. He must be sad that he does not have any children, because he can be a very grumpy old cuss. That makes me a little bit scared to ask him questions—I must. Maybe I can follow him around in secret until I find out if he is a war profiteer.

The Trey o' Hearts

*A*ugust 4, 1918

This war has made me worried, worried so much of the time. But I always feel joy—not grief or worry—when I am reading my library books. I do not think about the war then! I just read *The Trey o' Hearts*, which was written in 1914 for the purpose of making a silent moving picture from the story. They made the moving picture in the same year, 1914, before the war had really started. The moving picture took over two thousand feet of film and was directed by Mister Wilford Lucas.

Theater

I am still thinking about the beautiful Rose Trine from the book. She was in love with Alan Law, and his mighty heart loved her back. She always wore roses on her belt. She told Alan that if she loved him, she would send him a rose. Everywhere Alan went, there was a rose waiting for him! But there was also a playing card—the three of hearts—which means death!

One day, Alan received so many playing cards that he was afraid, so he ran away from England. Evil old Mister Trine ordered Rose's twin sister Judith to bring Alan back, dead or alive. Judith was evil, so she agreed to do it!

When Alan was in Canada, he was certain he saw Rose—but that is because he saw Judith, the twin sister! Finally Rose found Alan and fell sobbing into his arms. They escaped in a canoe, with Judith following and shooting her rifle at them the whole time.

There were many more adventures and scary things—but in the end, Alan married Judith instead of Rose! I could not believe it. He got mixed up, because Rose got killed. I think this is the saddest story in the world.

It is so nice to read a book and forget that war is everywhere. Even if the story is sad, it is not as sad as our brave soldiers dying every day. I hope our gunpowder is helping them blast the enemy back to Germany!

Buck Private McCollum

August 12, 1918

Buck Private McCollum is from Huntington, West Virginia. He is in France fighting in the war and writing rhymes while he is there. His sister lives here in Nitro, and she showed me his letters and poems. His letters help his mother wait for him to return from the war.

She made a book of the poems to be proud of when he comes home from war. She called the book *History and Rhymes of the Lost Battalion* because he wrote the rhymes while a battalion was lost in the Argonne Forest.

The rhymes are an inspiration—they show that the Buck Private can have courage at the same time as fear, and he believes in his Major Whittlesee very much.

I believe I have the soul of a writer and a poet. Maybe I am like the Buck Private.

It is important for mothers to write to their sons who are soldiers even if the letters are terribly sad because the mothers miss their sons very much. If every soldier gets words of encouragement they can stay strong and courageous while they fight the war.

I copied out one letter:

My brave boy,

Always there are days I am thinking of you. I could
scarcely believe otherwise for everywhere I see the call:
"Enlist, your country needs you." I know that you
have heeded that call and somewhere, under orders,
you are wearing your country's uniform and bearing
your country's arms, following "Old Glory" on land
or sea, ready to give for your country's honor and
defense your last full measure of devotion.

And so, while you are ever in my thoughts and I miss
you sadly, I am trying to be a good soldier, too, and do
my share and bear my burden bravely and cheerfully.
As my soldier had expected his mother to do.

True as it is that this mother did not raise her boy to
be a soldier, neither did she raise him to be a coward
or a shirk. Though my heart is often heavy with the
thought of separation, I know full well the pride the
mother feels when she realizes that the laddie is bravely
giving his best to a holy cause.

I am praying and believing that it shall always be your
best that you will give and do, for remember, my boy,
that your country is worthy, and nothing less than
your best will answer as a gift for her.

Americans like to think of themselves as a great, brave,
strong nation, a defender of the maker, a friend to the

oppressed, dauntless in peril, mighty in war, merciful, just and generous, loving home and the gentle arms of peace rather than the tumult and slaughter of the battlefield.

But our nation is composed of units, and it is only as you and I—and all—build into our characters the qualities that make a nation truly great that our national ideal can be realized. As long as you serve under your country's colors, you represent to the world every good and noble thing that your nation stands for. I pray this truth may dignify your thoughts, govern your impulses, and ennoble your soul.

All over our land, mothers are praying for their sons as I pray for you, not that you may altogether be preserved from temptation, but that you may be enabled to withstand at all times the lure of enemies without and the stress of foes within the citadel of your own being, so that you may come off victor over your own self. "He that ruleth himself is greater than he that taketh a city."

And so, my boy, Mother loves to think of you as enduring all things as a good soldier, and coming home someday under banners proudly floating, marching gladly to the victorious strains of drums and bugles, looking the world in the face with eyes clear and unabashed, to look bold to a loyal heart, your mother, wife and child, or to offer to that other One who proudly awaits your coming, the unsullied love and honor of a stainless life.

And if it so be that in the fearful din of mortal strife you yield your last great sacrifice for your country, may you be able in that last supreme moment to remember that in all things you did your best and honored the mother who bore you and the country for which you die.

May God, our Father, have you in his keeping to guard and to guide you. And now, let Mother say to you, as in the days not so long ago when you went to school: Be a good boy.

Goodbye,
Mother

Lots of soldiers write rhymes, not just the Buck Private. Mister Hill taught us one:

Eight men went to mow a meadow
Seven men went to mow a meadow
Six men went to mow a meadow
Five men went to mow a meadow
Four men went to mow a meadow
Three men went to mow a meadow

Two men went to mow a meadow

One man and his dog went to mow a meadow.

So sad!

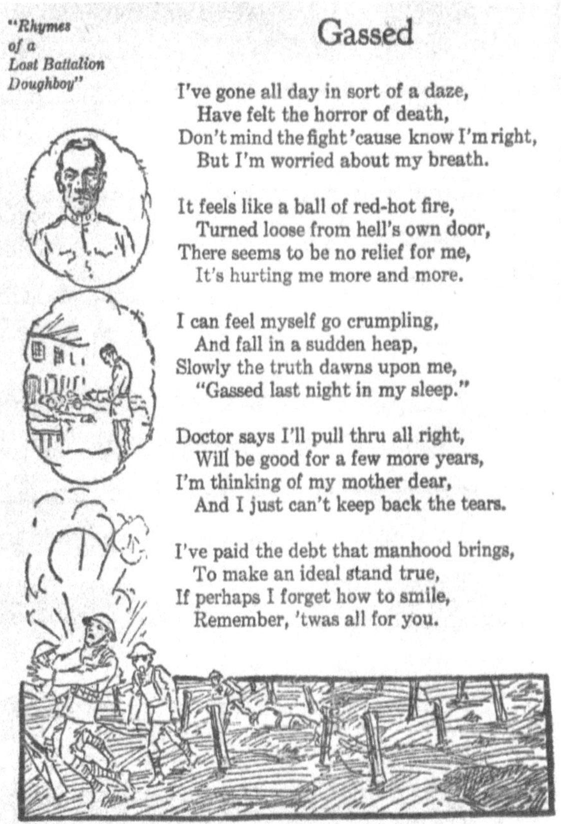

Gassed

I've gone all day in sort of a daze,
  Have felt the horror of death,
Don't mind the fight 'cause know I'm right,
  But I'm worried about my breath.

It feels like a ball of red-hot fire,
  Turned loose from hell's own door,
There seems to be no relief for me,
  It's hurting me more and more.

I can feel myself go crumpling,
  And fall in a sudden heap,
Slowly the truth dawns upon me,
  "Gassed last night in my sleep."

Doctor says I'll pull thru all right,
  Will be good for a few more years,
I'm thinking of my mother dear,
  And I just can't keep back the tears.

I've paid the debt that manhood brings,
  To make an ideal stand true,
If perhaps I forget how to smile,
  Remember, 'twas all for you.

"Gassed" by Buck Private McCollum

Each time we look at the names of the hospital patients we understand that everyone here is a soldier too. This makes us very proud but
sad at the same time. Sometimes I wish I was not a war correspon-

dent—when I cannot go to Ann's house or Abigail's house to work on our *Chronicles*, I have time to play like I did before this terrible war.

Tonight I will try to write poetically about my playtime.

> Just before the moon begins her promenade, wearing her regal shining tiara of stars or her bridal veil of fluffy clouds, and while dusk is changing windowpanes to black eyes, we go out to play.

Our farm has a rope swing that can spin its rider over a muddy bank, and we pretend that it is deadly quicksand down below. We pretend we are Tarzan sometimes, or the Druids that Mother told us about—from a long time ago in Scotland.

Their purpose was to conserve knowledge, so these stories were interesting to me—a war correspondent! They combined knowledge with religion and nature and believed in coming back to life. I wanted to play Druid and make potions like sacred water and a ceremony for a dead squirrel I found in the woods. If we bury the squirrel in a mason jar, we can learn later if the squirrel really has a soul. A broken jar or a missing lid could signify the escape of the soul from the grave. If there is no soul, there would not be a change to the jar.

In my Druid game my name is Sabrina, and I call our creek the Severn River like the river in Mother's stories. I will choose magical ingredients like twigs from an oak tree—some lucky wildflowers like nettles and honeysuckles and holly. Graveyard weed sounds unlucky, so it will not be used in our rituals. We will bless the trees and the flowers to make a perfect spot for the Druid burial—has to take place just after dusk.

I wrote a ceremony for the ritual and told everybody to set it to memory before we bury the squirrel:

> The river rushes to join its soul—dip one hand into
> the Severn River
> Mistletoe promises uniting—wave holly three times
> over the squirrel
> The roots of the pulpit can never be known—bow
> twice to the High Druid—ME!
> The scythe can slash open the dark—at this time I will
> SLASH!
> We await the burst of the soul—everybody might cry
> at this time

***

Well—it did not turn out like I hoped it would. Ellen stood still for the ritual but she talked the whole time to Ruby Lips—her pretend friend. John Dominique came—he splashed us with water from the Severn and put a holly sprig up his nose. I do not know why he even came. In the last part of the ceremony I took a small tree branch and covered the mason jar with dirt from the creek. I swear right now that I will never return to look for the soul. That squirrel will rest in peace.

A Party

*A*ugust 14, 1918

Before school starts up I am thinking that I must have a party to keep our spirits high! And I will do some war teaching at the party—so that we learn and have fun at the same time.

You are driving your ducks to a poor market Mother will say. Nobody really wants to learn more about the war. They just want to go watch the men in the boxing ring at the barracks! But I am going to teach anyway. I have the plan in my brain. We will have the party in the dry part of the field—not in muddy pastures. No mud means no mud pies—we are getting too old to care about that!

We can play "Mother may I?" because everybody loves that game. Somebody asks Mother, may I take two steps toward the finish line? And Mother—that will be me—says: You may if you can name the President of the United States of America. If they ask to take more steps, I will come up with harder questions: What ammunition do we make here? Name our enemy in the Great War. Do you know what war profiteering is? I will have to come up with a wonderful prize for the winner. Daddy will say fresh eggs, but that is not a real prize.

And if we play musical chairs—I can decorate a special chair for the winner! We need music for musical chairs, but I can figure that out later. Maybe I can borrow the triangles from our school. We could do a cakewalk too! Then we'll play tag and sack race and hot potato—a wonderful party!

None of the city kids know how to ride horses, but maybe I can ask Mister Lanier if we can borrow his pony Swizzle for safe rides. Ponies can be mean, but I am good with horses so I will lead Swizzle.

I am so very proud of our farm, but most of the city kids have not ever been here except for Noble—he lived here before we were called a boomtown and called Nitro. And also of course Ann and Abigail came here the day we met last year. I am worried that the city kids will be sad that our farmhouse does not have a toilet room. And I am worried about Mother—she will surely try to get everyone to sing something like "Amazing Grace" or play an old-fashioned game like ring around the rosie. I will be strong and tell her NO! I am old enough to make my own party.

A party is just what we need to keep our spirits high during the war! I will make lemonade, and Mother will make little cakes for the cake walk. She will want to make her special blackberry or rhubarb pies, but I will ask very nicely for teacakes with frosting. You cannot put frosting on a rhubarb pie!

I will invite Ann and Abigail and even Elise and Emmaline if they are not too mean to me. Noble can come, and Andrew and Kevin and Bucky even though I have not forgotten how mean they were about the devil duster and the snowman. If I invite Camille, Marty, Karen, Wilma, Cathy, and Carolyn, we will have enough people for a game of tug of war! Carla and Cindy and Melissa are pretty nice too. I can even invite Cat—we call her that because she is very quiet and good at climbing trees—even if she did not want to help us with *The Victory Chronicles*. There are so many children in Nitro now!

I will make beautiful invitations. I read the proper way to write them from the *Future Perfect* book. I must send them out at least five

days before the party like a friendly letter. Then the guests answer the
invitation with their own letter. I will write them like this:

> Mother says I may have an outdoor party. I do hope
> you will come. It will be on Saturday, August 24th
> from two o'clock until four o'clock, at Ana Ariano's
> big farm. There will be games and prizes!

My Special Party

August 24, 1918

My special party was a wonderful success! All the girls came a little bit early so we could play Daisy Loves Me before the boys get here. Every girl picks a wild daisy—these are everywhere in August. When she picks one petal off, she says he loves me. On the next petal, she says he loves me not. When she gets to the last petal she will find out if her sweetheart loves her or not! My last daisy said he loves me, but I do not have a sweetheart.

Only some of the boys came—not Noble—but once they got here we played "Mother may I?" My questions were all about Nitro and the war. I even let Sarah and Ellen play. Everyone knew the answers to most of the questions, even—When are walnuts ready? Where is Devil's Tea Table? Some were stumped by the tougher questions like—How much does the train fare cost?

Mother told me to play ring around the rosie but I said NO. We used old feed bags for a sack race. I lost, but only because Andrew snuck a rock into my feed bag. Then we played tag.

Kay won the cakewalk—Mother had baked a beautiful chocolate cake with frosting for her prize. Mario cheated at hot potato so NO-BODY really won.

Everyone liked the lemonade but nobody wanted to ride Swizzle. I promised to lead him gently around the pasture, but the city kids were afraid that he might be mean. One time he leaned so hard against Sarah in the barn that we thought she would be crushed against the wall! And Howard told everyone that Swizzle crushed a man to death once even if Shetland ponies are not nearly as big as horses. After that my plan was ruined once and for all—nobody would take a ride.

Everybody had fun and they wanted to stay longer, but Mother said it was time for chores. I told them I never have chores.

I think our spirits were lifted much higher!

Trucks and Cars
Take Our Place

September 1, 1918

Today I am feeling like I have not done enough for America in war or ever because I have been worried about Mother and Daddy and horses and the last century—I left a very important part of the war effort out of *The Victory Chronicles*.

I know we are doing a lot here in Nitro, and we can make our share of five hundred thousand pounds of gunpowder each day to push back our enemies the Germans. My family saves food—growing squash and cucumbers and green beans here on our farm. We save the grain for the horses and do not eat meat on certain days so that there is more for the soldiers.

Across all of America every time the call goes out for more fighters, more brave men go to war and many women go to be nurses and factory workers. There are millions and millions of soldiers fighting in the war. I heard that there are over one million just in France!

Ann and Abigail and I are still working hard as war correspondents to the President—copying down valuable information for our *Victory Chronicles* and making sure that it is safe and only for the eyes of the Secretary of War and the President. This is our most important work to help the war effort.

I missed one of the most important new war facts because of how much I love horses. I cannot tell this new fact to Mother and Daddy because it has to do with hauling by trucks instead of our oxen. The Heavy Haulage Company in New York will furnish trucks for hauling—sandstone and gravel and lumber—all around the plant. There will be fifty-two trucks, forty-five rear-dumping trucks, and three side-dumping trucks. The oxen will still help haul machinery and move houses, but most of the work will be done by trucks now.

Garage at Explosives Plant C

I cannot bear to tell Mother and Daddy this news. What if I am the first to tell them? Will we have to move somewhere else? Will anyone still need an oxen team? John already said he wants to move to Ohio after the war. Maybe we will all go with him. I hope there is still a pasture wherever we go next. If they say I cannot take Mabel and Circle C with me then I am staying right here. I promise this to myself right now. I know how to run our farm—even how to use the tiller with Mabel pulling it!

I have seen the cars and trucks at the plant garage. Maybe I am not so smart after all—I did not realize until today that the trucks are taking our place and locomotives are taking the place of our horses. Mister Moody told us this would happen. I think I understand now why Daddy looked so serious after the engineers came last year. I hope somebody tells Daddy how he can get started on new modern work.

Automobiles, like the jalopy shown here, rose quickly in popularity.

I am dreaming of the end of the war when Ann and Abigail and I get to go to Washington, D.C., to sit beside President Wilson at a grand banquet for everybody who has done important war work.

A Nasty Note

September 14, 1918

Ann wrote a nasty note and gave it to me today.

You are borrowing way too many papers from my daddy, and he is getting very angry because he needs them right away. You have messed up everything. I am in bad trouble. I may have to tell on you. You must return everything you have borrowed including all the pictures. BEWARE AND TAKE CARE.

Sorry you are a correspondent—maybe

Ann

Ann can be very cruel—I know she does not mean it. Abigail gave me the note but she said she did not read it first or show it to anyone else. I bet she is lying!

All night long this has made me think of the story *Ruth Fielding at Lighthouse Point* by Alice B. Emerson. Mary Cox was always mean in the book, but Ruth stayed strong and brave.

Noble Is Another Friend!

September 23, 1918

I have a very important piece of paper to carry around with me today and always—it was NOBLE's great idea! We are now certain that Noble was right about the war profiteers.

I used to make fun of Abigail's arithmetic sums because they kept coming out different, but now I know it was not her fault. I am very sorry for being harsh, and I will beg her to forgive me. We realized that the sums for the money spent on supplies like platinum do not add up right because there must be war profiteering going on! When she saw one sum reporting fifty million dollars were needed, and Mister Martin told her seven hundred seventy-seven million dollars, we should have figured out right then that something was wrong. Abigail's arithmetic could not have gotten her that confused.

Noble had Abigail write about our dangerous situation—truthfully and completely so that if we ever run into some real trouble from the war profiteers, everybody will know what happened to us. She will write three copies—one for me, one for Ann, and one for Noble—so that the war profiteers will not be able to get us without getting caught!

My name is Abigail Palmer and I live in Nitro, West Virginia. I came here with all my family to help in a war emergency for the United States. My daddy is a chemical engineer.

The farmers and scientists are working together here to build a modern gunpowder plant in only ten months. We will make enough gunpowder to win this awful war against the Germans.

My friends and I have been writing *Victory Chronicles* to send to President Woodrow Wilson with important information and reports from here in Nitro so that he can follow our war progress. I do the sums and averages because I am the best at arithmetic—even long division! But when I was gathering all of these numbers together, I realized that no matter how hard I try, the different reports have different numbers. This makes us certain that war profiteering is happening right here in Nitro. The sums are not adding up!

We are afraid that we are in grave danger because of what we now know. The war profiteers may be coming after us already. I have written three copies of this letter. One for Ana Ariano, one for Ann Moody—these two are war correspondents like me—and one for our friend, whose name I will not say. He will keep the letter safe even if Ann or Ana loses it. He has been on our side from the start, warning us about the danger but we did not believe him until now. Well, we should have been as smart as him all along, and now we have to hope that we do not get kidnapped and locked up in the tunnel Mister Muck built underneath his house.

Officially signed,
Abigail Palmer

Abigail is so loyal and smart—I should have believed her when she promised that she was reporting the right numbers. Well, the truth is out now—war profiteering is here in Nitro!

I am putting my trust in Noble. He has been a true friend trying to save us from the start. I know now that he really does know the truth—I do not know how, but war profiteers and spies must be watching us and wondering how much we know. I feel very guilty for being a smarty pants to Noble and Abigail, and I must make it up to them.

Should we write about this to President Wilson, or should we try not to worry him? Who can we go to for help? Well, no matter what happens, our hopes for victory are still higher than the tallest transformer at the plant!

Dot-to-Dot Puzzle

September 29, 1918

Victory is the only thing that will make me a whole person with a whole heart again. We can do this—I believe it. I will not be brokenhearted forever!

Yes, victory is like the dot-to-dot puzzles I love so much. There are so many parts in war, and they all have to be connected together to make victory. Even if the page looks like a useless collection of dots, if you follow the numbers you will have a spring lamb!

I can make a dot-to-dot puzzle about Nitro's war effort right now. Here are the dots:

1. Falling rain

2. Lump of black coal

3. Cloud of gas

4. Electric pole

5. Spying glass

6. Brave horse

7. One million dollars—on a golden crown!

8. Devil duster

9. Train engine

10. Ammunition box

11. Telephone

12. Nurse cap

13. Fire truck

14. Noble's house

15. Missus Funston

16. Daisy game

17. Rhubarb stalk

18. American flag

19. History schoolbook

20. Harry's snake

Connect all the dots—VICTORY!

School Will Not Open on Time

*O*ctober 12, 1918

I thought every bad thing that could happen had already happened to us with war profiteering and everything, but I was wrong. Now our brand-new school will not open on the right day! It should have already opened, but it is not all ready yet. It is important for it to open so that the children will have somewhere to go while their mothers and daddies are working. There will also be a night school for grownups.

Ann and Abigail and I are so excited for our new lessons—like sewing and spelling and penmanship and arithmetic and art and music. Mother could be the sewing teacher! Missus Marsh will still be a teacher at our school. I will like geography and hygiene class.

We are singing a new song Ann taught us:

Readin' and writin' and 'rithmetic

Taught to the tune of the hick'ry stick

You were my queen in calico

I was your bashful barefoot beau

You wrote on my slate

I love you so

When we were a couple of kids!

Maybe we can sing this song for all the other pupils at the new school. I bet Noble will sing it to Elise—she will not like that!

Daddy feels sorry that our school will not open on time, so he said we could take the third level of our beehive off. It is called the super, and it has all the extra honey that the bees do not need. They only ever use the first and second levels for food. We were not able to open it up before because we did not have the special hat with a screen or safe gloves. But now, Mother has made a face covering for us, and Daddy bought gloves at the general store. We will open the hive and feast on delicious honey!

We will go to the bees when it is nearly dark so they will have settled down for the night. We can puff the smoker to calm them down even more. Then we open up the super and cut the honey blocks out. I hope I will not get stung, but I am looking forward to the honey. Clover honey is the best, but other flowers make for good honey too. If the honey is from clovers, it will be light yellow color.

***

We got to the honey and Mother cut it out. The bees will fill the super back up again soon.

Ellen was too scared of getting stung so she backed out before we even started—but with Daddy keeping us safe nobody got stung.

We will save some of the honey for winter, which will make winter so much better.

Our new school will not teach the pupils how to get honey, so I want to teach Ann and Abigail how. Elise and Emmaline, too! But I already know Mother will say no, it is too dangerous for my friends.

When our new school opens all the children will study there, but the colored children will have to go to a different school. They are saying it will be just as good. I hope so. I do not understand why they cannot just build a school big enough for everybody.

Daddy showed us a picture of a school in Poca, West Virginia, where Mister Lanier's grandfather went. Daddy wanted us to appreciate how important schooling is. Our new school will be very modern—will not teach all of the farm ways I learned from Mother and Daddy. But I think both old school ways and new school ways are important!

West Virginia schoolhouse, 19th century

Tonight I want to make sure I honor Veway H. Cook before I go to sleep. We hear that he will never be coming back from France. I pay tribute to his bravery and courage. He wrote on the inside of his gas mask:

LIKE A BABY NEEDS
ITS MOTHER
FORSAKE ME NEVER
FAIL ME NEVER

Good night I pray the Lord my soul to keep!

Nobody Likes Me

Our new school is almost ready, so we had a day of lessons today even if we will not really start until November 25. I did not want to go today. I do not believe anybody likes me. When I was starting to swing out on the rope swing a few days ago Tony came over and seemed very angry with me.

Your meddling got my daddy in trouble. A touring car got stolen, and because he works at the mechanic garage he got in big trouble! He got so mad he shoved me over the bank before I was ready to swing out, and I scratched my knee badly when I landed. But I did not cry—not when he could see me!

I will get praise for my work when the war is over. Mister Baker will invite us to a victory banquet. I am so glad Mother showed me which spoon is for dessert, and now I know what a gravy boat is so I will be ready for another fancy supper.

I have to remember *The Trey o' Hearts* in times like this. Brave Alan Law married the wrong girl. Life does not turn out good all the time, and it can be hard to forgive people who have done us wrong. But then I also remember *Ruth Fielding at Lighthouse Point*. Ruth Fielding always forgave, even when Mary Cox the Fox tried to hurt her. I will try to forgive Tony, but it would be almost impossible to forgive if someone tried to kill war correspondents—like us or Anna Steese Richardson.

I am pretty sure the other pupils do not like me. It is clear when we play war. They always make me be the German—so I have to get tied up. Then they try to make me drink pokeberry juice, which is poison. Larry says it tastes good like a persimmon—it looks just like grape juice—but I am too smart to get it mixed up with grape juice.

Sometimes the boys make cigarettes to smoke from corn silk. They make an awful smell. I hope Mother never hears about the boys making cigarettes! I would never smoke a cigarette—not even three puffs.

I must study President Wilson's Fourteen Points peace plan, which he told everybody in a speech in January. It is very difficult for me to understand, but I will work hard.

Another Day

November 5, 1918

I still do not want to go to school.

Mother told me to be bold—she does not know about everything that has happened to me this summer. I fully admit we told the police to call Mister Fields to the station and ask him about collecting rent for the free houses. But I am not the reason Mister Mudd was let go, and I never lied about Mister Muck's tunnel. I saw it once when we were up at Devil's Tea Table. And I did see real platinum. Still, everyone thinks I am a meddlesome liar.

You think you are a High Druid—from Gary. You think your made-up ceremonies make the river magic, and your soul will come back to life.

Dreamer girl! You will never be a dream girl—Andrew added in. You dream that a brave knight on a magnificent horse will ride into war and save you from murder! Nobody seemed to remember that Andrew put a rock in my grain sack at my party so I could not win the sack race. He is a cheater!

Besides, I am only doing my assignment as a war correspondent when I follow Mister Raines around to find out if he is a war profiteer. Maybe I can change my name to Laura or Lurlene—people can call me Lee—and everyone will forget about Ana and all the reasons they do not like her.

Jane Delano pictured on a Red Cross
pamphlet

They will all be so sorry if we really get killed. They will remember
the help we gave the President! I bet if I sprained my ankle they might
want to be friends again.

Well, I have some more things to write down before chores.

I always get a U for Unsatisfactory in penmanship. Elise and Emmaline always get an S+ for Extra Satisfactory. Ann and Abigail make good marks in everything. It feels like I have to work twice as hard as them at school.

In our copybooks today we had to write about our favorite flower. I picked daffodils. Noble picked the Venus flytrap. We recited what we wrote, and Noble got in trouble. I knew he would!

I did learn more about President Wilson's Fourteen Points peace plan. I think talks about peace started just around the time we started building Plant C here in Nitro in December last year. The peace plans did not go through—so the war goes on.

I also read about Jane Delano—one of the bravest nurses in the war. She helped lead the Red Cross and the Army Nurse Corps. There are over eighteen thousand nurses working overseas. Hundreds have died in the war. I will honor Jane Delano by using her name to help me remember the President's requirements for a peace agreement.

This will help me remember some of our President's brilliant plans for peace. Some countries are not happy about this—especially the Germans. They do not want to pay money for all the damage they have caused. Some of them feel they have been stabbed in the back. People who do not want peace are called fire-eaters. We are not fire-eaters, that is for sure.

J: Justice for Brave Little Belgium and France

A: Agreement for territories and no trading land around

N: National arms weapons reduced for Germany

E: Equality of other trade among the countries

D: Democracy for all

E: Equal and fair borders for Italy

L: League of Nations to band together and always work for peace

A: Autonomous development in Turkey

N: Navigation freedom

O: Open seas

Marshmallow

November 6, 1918

I told Noble about my memory trick using Jane Delano's name to remember the Fourteen Points for peace. He is going to try the same thing, but he will use a different name than Jane Delano. He says he might try Missus Marsh, our own teacher, but add Mallow to make it longer. Marshmallow! Sometimes Noble can be funny.

John asked what we were working on and laughed out loud when we told him. He said YWF—You Will Forget!

Schoolteacher with pupils

Here is Noble's trick:

M: Make no land trades

A: Agree on land boundaries

R: Reparations

S: Some people are fire-eaters because they are not happy about peace

H: Happiness if all countries could just agree on no more wars

M: Make democracy for all

A: Allow Belgium to get help

L: League of Nations forms

L: Large and small countries work together

O: Open seas

W: Weapons reduced

Noble is a true friend now.

Keith

November 6, 1918

My great hope is that when the war ends all my friends will like me again. My special party this summer did not help. I have lost all my friends except Ann and Abigail. The others are not as mean to Ann and Abigail as they are to me. Noble is always nice to Abigail.

Just yesterday, Charles poured the ink out of his inkwell into my book satchel. He was not even sneaky because he wanted me to know he did it. My book satchel has many of my private rhymes, and they were all ruined.

At least I am not the only one people are mean to. People call Keith Old Man River because he is big and wide. He has not come to school for two days in a row. I should have asked him to my special party but I did not know then how it feels to not have any friends.

Armistice

November 7, 1918

Today, November 7, is the most important day of my life. Missus Marsh told us that an armistice has been signed! Hooray!

It is important not to get excited she always says. But not today! Everybody was so excited, and the classroom got noisier and noisier. Mary Jane even got out of her seat to go over and hug her fast friend and Louis tapped on his desk with a pencil like he was playing a drum. I could hear the church bell ringing outside and when I looked out the window there were people dancing and singing on the street. Ivy started crying tears of joy because her daddy works in one of the acid plants.

Missus Marsh let us square dance right after lunch—we hardly ever get to. The boys were even allowed to play mumbletypeg in the schoolyard with their pocketknives. I wanted Bucky to lose because the loser has to pull out all of the pocketknives with his teeth.

Now remember children, there is still much work ahead—Missus Marsh told us when we were back inside. All the different countries will have demands, and everyone has to reach an agreement before there is a final peace treaty.

I hurried home to tell Mother and Daddy the wonderful news. Mother was fixing supper, but she said she and Daddy had already heard about it. That is why she was frying chicken—a special celebration! They let us dance around even if Methodists do not believe in dancing.

It is past bedtime now but I am just remembering all the work everybody did on the way to victory. My most important work was *The Victory Chronicles*, especially because it helped me warn the police about war profiteering. And I joined the pin-money club to earn money for the war.

There were other things like not having sugar in our candy. We had meatless Mondays and gasless Tuesdays and sometimes no electric lights. We grew food in our gardens so there was more food to send to the fighting soldiers.

In Nitro we started to make gunpowder for our soldiers. We hauled timber—shared our beds and our attics and basements with the new workers and we built a boomtown in a big hurry.

I even heard that Missus Wilson let sheep graze in the front yard of the White House in Washington. The soldiers needed wool for socks and sweaters! Like they say in the magazines—we sure did knit our bit!

I could not be happier. Victory is here!

A Cruel Hoax

November 8, 1918

I was almost late to my lessons today because Mother forced me to eat oatmeal—I hate oatmeal!

When I got there I saw Missus Parsons standing in the schoolyard all by herself. She looked like she was crumbling away. Her head was down and she was bent low. Daddy calls it lowdown when people look like this. I thought she was probably sad because she has to teach the second-form children—my joke—too mean Ana!

As soon as I went inside Missus Marsh told us the news about the armistice was only a cruel hoax. No one knows how this false report happened. It might have come from France or Germany. I had never seen Missus Marsh cry but she was crying today along with everybody else.

Keep believing in Nitro's gunpowder—it will just be a little longer until we win.

Then she made us start our lessons, even if our hearts were broken! We learned about the great history of Nitro. Before Plant C, before even our farming village, this land was claimed by King George of England in 1773. It was around this area that George Washington did the Pocatalico Survey. We know about this. He carved G and W into a tree somewhere.

Missus Marsh wanted to teach us about all the help children give to the war effort. We got out our copybooks to copy down facts—maybe an oral exercise tomorrow. She said we should be able to recite five facts. I hope I study hard enough tonight.

- Children in London, England, went out encouraging men to enlist.

- Some children in Russia enlisted even if they were too young.

- Schoolboys joined the Officer Training Corps to learn how to be leaders on the front lines.

- Schoolgirls planted gardens and raised money to buy pigs for their schools.

- The Boy Scouts in Britain handed out food, scrubbed floors, and passed messages along to the families of missing soldiers.

- Girl Guides in Britain rolled up bandages and sewed clothes.

- Children picked scrap metal out of rubbish heaps to save for the war.

- Captain Ball, who was only seventeen when he enlisted, shot down forty-three German airplanes before he got killed.

She did not say anything about *The Victory Chronicles* or that we were war correspondents. I did not say anything.

After lunch the schoolroom was very quiet. Old Man River did not stomp around Bucky's desk, and James Rotten Totten did not grab hold of his throat and act like he was sick. Larry did not try to pour ink out of his pen onto anybody's desk. It is very unusual for the schoolroom to be this quiet.

It was so quiet that I took the opportunity to ask everybody to please call me Lurlene from now on. But then the boys got mean and said I should be called Jane Plain.

Enough! Then we heard—today, we have to look to the future—a future when all of this suffering has ended. It was Elise who had stood up beside her own desk! She went on—we all have a mission to help in the war. Look at the work Ana and Ann and Abigail have done being war correspondents. Have you worked this hard for the war effort?

Then Emmaline took up for me also! I was so surprised and a little bit guilty because I had not tried hard enough to be their friend.

As it turns out, they have both been looking for spies in secret. They hid in Mister Hayes feed store and Mister McCallister's pet store to listen for clues! It is true I should have been kinder. They made the best Buy War Bonds posters, and they love all creatures great and small. They are the only ones who do not get annoyed about Harry's snake.

Then Missus Marsh came in, and we had to get out our copybooks and she spoke about the end of the war. Children will no longer have to lie about their age to join the army. They can just go back to their own homes. And there will be no more homes in tents for that matter! The French will no longer have to hide from air raids, and they can eat bread and butter again. There will not be a single more bomb on Christmas Eve. We copied down as fast as we could. Missus Marsh was talking fast.

Then she had us copy down some of our own ideas. This made me a little worried that people would try to be funny and show off. But people wrote things like no more sewing or knitting for soldiers, and no more big gardens to save food for everybody. This made me a little sad because I like our garden. Eric said there would be no more dog fights—this is when airplanes fight up in the sky. No more spies and no more making dangerous gunpowder.

Then it was back to our usual lessons. We worked on page eighteen of *A Practical English Grammar*. My notes:

Interjections may express:

1. Joy: Hurrah!
2. Pain or suffering: Alas! Oh!
3. Surprise: What! Ha!
4. Disapproval: Fudge! Hie!
5. A call for attention: Hey! Ho! Hark!

This book is pretty old, but I suppose nothing much has changed since it was written. We will probably have another oral exercise about this lesson. Alas! I am undone. There, I used another interjection!

Next year it will be technical grammar. I hope it is not too hard.

Sassy Class

*N*ovember 12, 1918

I went to school today feeling very sad again. Abigail said no more *Chronicles* because the war is almost over. Ann wants to move away right away. I cannot remember what else anybody else said because I was busy trying to look joyful even if I was hurting inside.

I may have to keep you a little later today, Missus Marsh told us. The room broke out in whispers—she never did this before. What is this about? Was somebody getting punished? Who? What for? I wanted to know. It could not be a party, because that is never allowed. Missus Marsh will not let us bring sweets for birthdays, even if they always have birthday parties in Missus Parsons' classroom. We can hear them. It makes Missus Marsh very angry.

Missus Parsons gets in trouble all the time—maybe even more than a pupil. Sometimes she lets her pupils go home before it is even time. One time her whole class got to go to Mister Lanier's farm to see his new calf. When it was time to leave Peggy Louise had gone missing! They looked for her in the barn and everywhere. It turned out she just walked home by herself.

Take out your copybooks please—Missus Marsh.

I ain't got my copybook today—Bucky never speaks in proper English. We all laughed to try to ease our minds.

The English lesson for today was about adjectives, which give more meaning to nouns. We copied down a paragraph that uses many adjectives.

> The soldiers wear <u>strict</u> uniforms. They have to carry their <u>heavy</u> backpacks and equipment, which weigh over ninety pounds. They carry a <u>big</u> cot, a <u>small</u> trench shovel, a <u>powerful</u> gun that can shoot in .07 seconds, and a <u>heavy</u> load of ammunition. They need water, so they always carry a canteen and a mess kit with a spoon, a fork, a <u>small</u> plate, and <u>little</u> tins of food. They always need <u>thick</u> socks and <u>sturdy</u> boots. Soldiers have to fight in the <u>muddy</u> trenches.

I could not believe the cruel things the other students said about Missus Marsh when she went to get the triangle. Her face does not look like a marshmallow! And they should be careful because we will have her as our teacher again next year. But they did not want to stay late.

The boys were making plans so that we could go home. Bobby was going to make himself vomit. Old Man River planned to yell out that he had to go play piano right when school lets out. That was funny! Larry was going to pretend he still did not understand adjectives and could Missus Marsh please explain them again, and maybe she would forget to keep us late!

Nobody did any of those things. We sat very quiet for our history lesson.

After lunchtime she let us play the fortune teller game with special cards. The playing cards have pictures of ducks and lambs and haystacks. Everybody got a turn. She said we should guess if the war might be over for real this time or if we will be famous someday. If you get three cards of the same kind, the answer is yes!

But at three o'clock, we still could not go home. We stayed quiet, but I know everyone was annoyed. Then she told us the wonderful news—peace had arrived! She wanted to wait until she was absolutely sure this time before she told us.

Victory train to Charleston that departed four days before actual victory was declared

Germany surrendered at last, and an armistice was signed on the eleventh hour of the eleventh day of the eleventh month of 1918, on a train car somewhere in France. Missus Marsh repeated that there was still a lot of work ahead. France is almost destroyed and many Americans are discouraged about the war.

Celebrations broke out again—just like last week. But this time it was real! All over America people are singing and dancing and filling up the streets. Hooray! But there is some sadness here in Nitro, because some people could not afford to get back on the train to go to Charleston for the big celebration. They had just gone four days ago because of the hoax—too soon to make the trip again!

Doubts

November 13, 1918

I am not sure what to believe in now. What if peace is not real again?

From all the bad times we have faced—deadly weapons, death, war profiteering, and all the rumors and lies—I do not think I can believe anything is the truth now or ever again. I believed the hoax about the war being over last week. I believed the rumor about typhoid fever, but it turned out NOT to be just a rumor. I believed Mister Mudd was a spy. I refused to believe that some people were war profiteers or spies even after Noble showed us their pictures. And those rumors were real after all.

Is it even true that the great flu this year will kill one half of one million people? People are too scared or too sick to go anywhere—women are still not allowed to vote? The war ended? Is all this really true?

I am writing more—a lot of things turned out to be true. A lot of things turned out not to be true. I am hoping it is NOT true when they say over fifty million people will have died in the war when it is all counted up.

I promise myself right now that I will be more careful about what I listen to. I will ask more questions—like when Daddy told me YES on the egg and spoon race with Mabel. I got so excited because Mabel is so sturdy—we would not drop the egg out of the spoon in a race. But then he told me NO I could not go in the race! I should have asked questions right then—she is not too big to run fast. She is sturdy and gentle! So why? With Mabel I would have won the race for sure.

When Missus Marsh said the first peace was a hoax but victory would still come very soon I did not believe it—even now I do not know what to believe.

Ann and Abigail are moving away from Nitro after the war ends. I hope this is just a rumor. Will there be enough new modern work for people to do here in Nitro? Will there be enough pupils to fill up our new school?

The school is real. I know that much—even if I do not trust myself.

I read *Rhymes of the Lost Battalion* to make myself feel better. The Lost Battalion did not die. They were lost somewhere in the Argonne Forest in France. They survived one of the most terrible battles of the war—more than twenty-six thousand other people died. Sometimes, what you thought was terrible turns out to have a happy ending—like finding the Lost Battalion.

I copied down this rhyme from the book. I love it because we are all buddies!

> From small a thing as "gimme a light"
> To laying down his life in a fight,
> There was no color, nor was there creed,
> Whenever a buddy was in need.
>
> —L.C. "Buck Private" McCollum

No New Modern Work

November 14, 1918

After we all got home today Daddy told Mother to gather all of us up at the supper table at five o'clock—he never does this. Mother only gathers us up when she tells us our chores. When Mother brought out the asparagus mixed with sauce and cheese I did not say one thing, even if I hate asparagus. I thought Daddy must want to tell us something important—he never talks very much.

There is no more work for me to do with Circle C or the horses—he sounded stern but sad all at the same time. He did not say more. He did not talk about working in the plant garage like a mechanic or a chauffeur or hauling supplies in trucks. He could not do that work because he does not know how cars and trucks work. There is no more timber for him to haul because the new haulage company can haul heavier loads. There is no work at Plant C now that the war is over—no need for train engineers here now.

Mother and Daddy really do see the future on its way now. I wanted to give out some of my ideas right then, but I knew better. Daddy looked too sad. We just went straight to our rooms after supper.

Ellen and Sarah went outside to play in the creek so I am all alone now and can write down my private thoughts. I cannot think about anything except Daddy's sadness right now. I am not sure if he will listen if I tell him about all the new modern work we could have if we keep becoming more modern and scientific here in Nitro. He listens to Mother mostly, but if he gets really mad at us for bothering him he might make up new rules for us to follow.

If anybody forgets to put the pitchfork away or leaves a saddle or bridle outside the barn, we have to shovel more manure! Or the tack room must be neat and tidy at all times. One time he made me take Ellen around with me for a whole day. John is old enough to know better than to bother Daddy with ideas so he never gets in trouble.

Surely a big dose of castor oil is good enough punishment, Mother sometimes says. Castor oil makes us all sick.

I am going to write a letter to Daddy about new modern work. I can put it in the barn and sign it like it is from Mister Lanier. Daddy only gets his pay on the days when he hauls—it is important for him to find work. Carpenters get sixty-two cents for every hour they work—up to eight hours, but sometimes they have to work for ten. Mister Hart gets forty cents every hour he works in the stables. Ann brags that her daddy gets around five hundred dollars every month—an engineer.

Dear Felice,

I believe you will like all the modern work coming to Nitro.

1. Collecting train tickets
2. Collecting tickets for the moving picture shows
3. Buying cows and sending milk to the new dairy—four thousand new gallons of milk every day
4. Working on the cars and trucks at the plant garage
5. Driving important people around in cars like a chauffeur

6. Loading up freight

7. Hauling fine timbers for more houses

8. Moving whole houses when they need to be moved

9. Laying down pipe for a new plant—just one section might need thirty-seven thousand feet of pipe

I know they will still need all of us here in Nitro. Missus Ariano can become a fine dressmaker. We will learn how to do all the new modern work that is coming our way.

Signed,

Mister Lanier

Daddy might still not listen but I tried!

I was so worried about Daddy and Mother's great sadness that I almost forgot to study my lessons. Today we had to copy down what a preposition is from the practical grammar book.

Preposition: One thing prepositions do is define relations. Write three sentences with prepositions. Write the preposition.

1. He died for his country. FOR

2. It was the night before Christmas. BEFORE

3. He stood on the bridge. ON

No prayers tonight. I wrote enough for one day!

Hygiene

November 16, 1918

We will be studying a new field called hygiene and there is a lot to learn. Missus Marsh told us about it and she will be our teacher. I already wash my brush and hair comb every Saturday night. I have to or I might get head lice like a lot of the other people. If we catch head lice from somebody's hair we have to wash our hair with pine-tar soap—stinky and sticky. I polish my shoes every week and iron my hair ribbons with a hot iron.

I always hang the clean wet clothes on the clothesline and bring it in at four o'clock when it is dry. Abigail says her mother always uses Lux soap sprinkling the flakes in the water to make them extra clean. And she has a special shampoo with coconut oil for shiny thick hair. Ann says her mother has Resinol Soap to keep her skin very beautiful. I saw the package—wash with soap, make a creamy lather, wash with more soap and splash with a dash of warm water. I think Abigail and Ann just like to brag about all their nice things.

Heaven Sends Down Clouds

November 27, 1918

When I started to get ready for school today I looked out my window and saw Daddy walking slowly to the barn carrying a bucket of grain in one hand and alfalfa tonic in the other to feed our team. But there were thick black clouds like storm clouds floating down from the sky and landing on the ground. Daddy dropped his bucket fast.

Mister Lanier was just standing around like he always does. I could see him through the clouds because his ugly head sticks up so high—supposed to help us around the farm but every time I see him he is just standing around. He is mean to Ellen—always tells her to get out of his way. He never brings Wilma and Paul over and I would like to play with them. One time I spit in his work boots after he left—that is true and I do not care who knows it!

It looked like Daddy was going to heaven through the storm clouds. I know he would do this for me and the rest of the family and wait for us there until we were all were dead and gone to heaven. He would do anything for all of us. Mister Lanier will definitely be going to the other place down below.

I knew I had to get to Daddy to see if he was okay. It could be a fire from the transformers making the black clouds.

I work my fingers to the bone, and what do I get? Bony fingers! Mother said when I ran through the kitchen. She always says that when we will not eat her griddle cakes with turnip lined in the bottom of the pan. Oatmeal is worse than rhubarb but griddle cakes are the worst of all. She must not have looked outside and seen the smoke. Breakfast was not important in this emergency! Sometimes she says—old blue Monday.

Daddy is on his way to heaven! I shouted out to Mother. I wanted to get to Daddy to say goodbye. I saw white birds flying over my head with bright red wings. A sure sign that Daddy was going to be taken to heaven!

On my way through the black clouds I heard shouts—Fire! Fire! I saw Daddy throwing buckets of water out of the pond onto one of the buildings.

The fire started in the night and is growing fast! I heard Mister Hart shouting this as he rode up on his horse Spitfire.

My mind was working fast. In Girl Scouts we learn how to start campfires and how to put them out—this fire looked much bigger than a campfire. The Girl Scouts motto is Courage, Confidence, Character. I know I can have courage, like when I saved our dog Buster from a coyote by getting him into the barn and closing the door lightning fast. But I did not have confidence this morning. I was not watching my feet and I tripped and fell right into a mud rut made by Mabel's big hooves. But courage was enough—muddy shoes would not stop me!

When I got closer I could see that the flying white birds were really burning paper. Electric volts ran through my brain I was thinking so fast. I could tell the fire was in the Administration Building where all of the secrets and plans are kept. There are thousands of important papers in there!

The fire wagon came right then with more water. I was so glad that we got the new fire wagon in April. And I was glad our *Victory Chronicles* might save whatever reports and pictures were burning up because we copied them down. It was good after all that we borrowed all those reports.

Ana, go home! Daddy yelled. I listened and started running back to the house. Sometimes I dream I am running so fast my feet do not even touch the ground. It is a good dream—I hate to wake up from it. Today I felt just like that and it was not in a dream!

Before I got all the way home Sarah and Ellen came running up to help. Noble was there too. He said he was right all along when he said Fire! Every time we played spies.

Spies have come to destroy all the evidence of war profiteering! Noble said this. I remember the pictures of spies he had showed us. Kate O'Hare got sent to prison for five years. Homer Spence planned riots against the war drafts in Oklahoma and got sent to prison for two years. Captain Franz von Rintelen even planted bombs. He got sent to prison for three years.

Spies must have come here to start the fire and then escaped down the river! We were told to be on the lookout for something like this. Mother's magazine *The Delineator* told us what to do. Do not wait to see if you are right or not. Report to the Department of Justice right away. You will not be told on for reporting something. Do not speak to anyone else because you might spread false rumors. Especially do not share any inside facts about where soldiers might be fighting.

President Wilson will need to know about this. Spies came here because our war work in Nitro! I am so thankful that Mister Baker was NOT here when the fire broke out. I almost hope he does not find out—but he will have to know.

Though never proven, the fire that burned down Explosives Plant C's Administration Building was suspected to have been started to destroy evidence of war profiteering.

More bad things are happening. The worst of all is that Mother's sister Aunt Vernie will come to visit. Mother always tells us to keep our wits about us and mind our manners when she is here. She must be more than one hundred years old—thinks she is the boss of us—tries to take charge and give advice. She will talk until the cows come home. She and Uncle Lester did not have any children so I think she wishes we were her own. She rides the train here from Point Pleasant. She makes us go out and pick flowers we can eat! In the summer and fall it is goldenrod and in the spring it is dandelions. Daddy says he has had dandelion wine.

When Aunt Vernie is not around we call her Aunt Skunk Cabbage. To make matters even worse, sometimes she brings her niece Carolyn. She is Aunt Vernie's favorite—not that I would want to be her favorite anyway! In the summer she makes me take Carolyn to Bible school with me. I hate Bible school. We go every day for two whole weeks instead of playing outside. But sometimes it is interesting, like when we learned about the whale that swallowed someone up whole—I think her name was Joan. But Joan got out somehow. Aunt Vernie never makes Carolyn go out to look for flowers. Is Carolyn my relation too? I am not sure—I will have to ask Aunt Vernie or Mother.

Poetry Contest

December 1, 1918

Peace is really here now. The horrible war is over! We will always remember that it ended on the eleventh hour of the eleventh day of the eleventh month in this year, 1918, in Paris, France. I feel like writing a happy rhyme to celebrate and honor everyone who fought so hard in so many different ways. This victory is for all of us!

I should enter the poetry contest in *The Delineator*.

We Are All Home Now

John Hively will be home
We no longer have to fight
We held up the right
We kept safe our USA
It was a long, long way to Tipperary

I understand that a lot of hard work still has to happen to decide the final terms for peace. I think there is plenty to celebrate for right now!

The Last Victory Chronicle

January 12, 1919

Dear President Wilson,

We are celebrating our great war victory with all of America. I must send you my last *Chronicle* today, along with a graph that shows our labor curve from the start to the end of war. We had the highest production in July, and then a slow shutdown began. I guess they thought the war would end sooner rather than later. All totaled we had 86,547 people working here to bring victory.

We all celebrated victory. Many people even went to Charleston to celebrate. But many people were so sad because they went to Charleston too soon because we heard the war was over before it really ended.

On January 15, 1919, after 380 days, we will shut down production for good. A fire destroyed the Administration Building with a lot of the reports and pictures inside, but engineers kept their drawings safe in big metal tubes. There will be more reports and pictures made over in 1919.

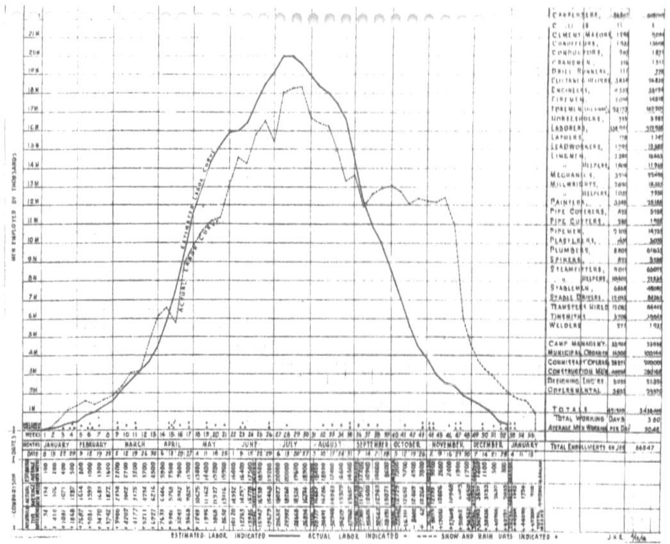

Labor chart. For enlarged image, see Appendix.

Munitions plants like the one here in Nitro had a lot of war profiteering. We are pretty sure that there were spies here and they worked with criminals to start the fire to hide war profiteering.

Now that it is time to look back and remember, I am sure that you will want to read about Buck Private McCollum from Huntington, West Virginia. He made a book of rhymes named *Rhymes of the Lost Battalion*.

I would also like to tell you about my brother John who could not fight because he is crippled by a twisted leg, but he wanted to help with all his heart. He helped Daddy with our oxen team in 1918 and worked in our gardens, because he could not help at the explosive plant. The work was too dangerous, and he would not be able to get away fast enough if there was an accident. It made him very sad. He has left Nitro now with his friend Dan to look for land to buy in Ohio or Kentucky. We are not certain where they will end up.

We know that we were united in our efforts and in our hearts for the United States of America! We are very proud of our country and of each other. Right out of our farmland we grew a new world of scientists and oxen drivers and horses and farmers and soldiers and civilians and doctors and nurses—all working together for victory. From farms to factories, two centuries happened in just one year!

I always knew we would win. And we will fight them again if we have to, and win again, too. But we have high hopes that the Peace Conference will achieve your Fourteen Points and that the League of Nations will be formed. Missus Marsh told us it would be very difficult at the conference—a lot of arguing between countries, but I know there will be a final peace. We all know that!

Thank you for leading us Mister President. We are sincerely proud to serve you and our country.

Signed your war correspondents,
Ana Ariano, Ann Moody, and Abigail Palmer

From Ann

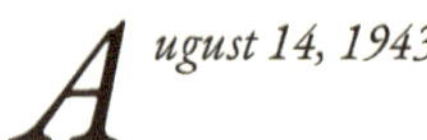

A ugust 14, 1943

Dearest Ana "Fresh Air" Ariano,

Today I am blue. I need to laugh and to remember what we did for America when we were only twelve years old in the Great War. I am using a typewriter to write this, which was so new when President Wilson sent a letter to Mildred White all those years ago.

Now the world is at war again against Germany and Japan. Ray and I are leaving immediately for Europe, where he will work in munitions and I will work as a war nurse just like my mother did. We will win the war this time too, I know it.

I will always be proud that our Nitro is an engineering marvel, famous like the Panama Canal. I will always believe that our work mattered and that we helped out in the war, even though we were children. I am sending some memories to you that mean a lot to

me: one of my mother's hospital records—partially
burned but saved from the rubble of the fire—and a
poster I bought showing children helping our country
in this latest war. I chuckled a little, remembering how
our own poster plans did not work out very well.

A poster from World War II

I want to send you the picture someone gave my father
after the fire, the four-room bungalow that was called
Type 182. It made me remember how devoted you

were back then to collecting all the plans and pictures. They had to make so many pictures and reports over again after the fire. Dad always saved that picture. Someone wrote on the picture: "This is a picture of our house dear. Isn't it a beauty? It is on the river overlooking the entire valley. I'll feel like a king. Keep this picture for me please." Dad thinks this was written some time around 1920.

Four-room bungalow for housing at Explosives Plant C

I was remembering today how it all happened. President Wilson realized it was so critical to produce massive amounts of gunpowder as quickly as possible, so he ordered our little village to work a miracle. We really did live in two centuries at the same time that year. We got so close in just nine months to make our share of five hundred thousand pounds of gun powder every day to send to war.

Do you still have some of those famous *Victory Chronicles*, maybe ones we forgot to send to President Wilson, or ones we rewrote before sending? We really were war correspondents for the United States! So many reports—ones we wrote, ones we copied, ones we borrowed, ones we sent, and some we lost! I remember it like it was yesterday.

As it turns out, we really did discover crimes of war profiteering. Munitions plants had the biggest problem with this during the war. So we were not wrong! We always thought it was Mister Raines whom you followed, or Mister Cunningham whom I followed. We thought we were in so much danger before and after the fire burned up so many records. The mystery of that fire was never solved. Maybe somebody really did want to keep us quiet. Good old Abigail was too good with figures. And Noble was not the world's biggest liar! Remember reading about Captain Eddie Rickenbacker, "The Flying Ace"?

Your mother always reminded us of duty, duty, duty. Your dad loved that awful drink Bevo. My parents drank the French 75, a cocktail named after the 77mm Howitzer machine gun. People drank rhubarb wine to save grain for the horses. And we learned about the devil duster and nitric acid. We were so jealous when Kevin and Andrew said they got into the plant.

I am so glad that I can tell people that I grew up in Nitro, West Virginia, and not "Redwop." What a name, huh? Nitro is much better. People probably don't know that Clark Gable worked on the power lines in Nitro in 1918 before he became a famous movie star for MGM. Or maybe this is just a rumor. Back in our reporting days we did create a lot of gossip.

I remember you cried so hard when you didn't know which section of houses they would let the Arianos live in if you got to move into town. You thought you might not get to be in the foreign-born section, even if your dad was born in Italy. I cried too because you might have to move farther away from my house than your farmhouse which was so nearby.

I know you remember how long it took to reach an agreement at the Peace Conference, just like Missus Marsh warned us. It took twelve leaders and months of negotiating to reach the final peace terms. Russia was left out because they were in the middle of a revolution. The negotiators really did not want to recognize Italy's frontier. Your ancestors! People thought President Wilson should not go to the conference since it might look weak, but he went of course. They couldn't even agree what language to speak at the negotiations, although they eventually settled on French and English.

So much happened. Poland declared independence. France wanted negotiators to tour France to show the complete destruction of their country, but they never did. Germany had to hand over ships in order to get food. Europe relied on us heavily for food. Lots of people thought Germany should pay money and be punished, but Germany said they had been betrayed and backstabbed by their own people.

President Wilson argued for what was most important to him—his Fourteen Points and the League of Nations. We studied these in school—you and Noble made a word trick, remember? Marsh + Mallow! That still makes me chuckle.

So many people died in that terrible war. Over ten million. We sent over one million American soldiers and nurses to the Great War. Over one million French soldiers died.

We thought everybody across the country was getting along, because that is how it was in Nitro. But this wasn't the case. Black people were tortured and murdered in cities like Chicago and Philadelphia, even though almost 400,000 Black men enlisted as soldiers. Taxes went up and gasoline was restricted. People complained about it a lot.

I remember you made me so jealous of your horse—I really did want a horse of my own! But you were right—there was no room in town to keep one. Did you hear that Newton Baker died in 1937?

Lots and lots of love,
Annie

P. S. F. Scott Fitzgerald wrote this in his novel *Tender Is the Night*: "This was a love battle ... All my beautiful lovely safe world blew itself up here with a great gust of high explosive love." Very true for us, right? Remember when David told Missus Marsh that he just sprinkled his commas around? Someday we will be together again in Nitro to remember it all over again. You used too many dashes and exclamations!!!

Appendix

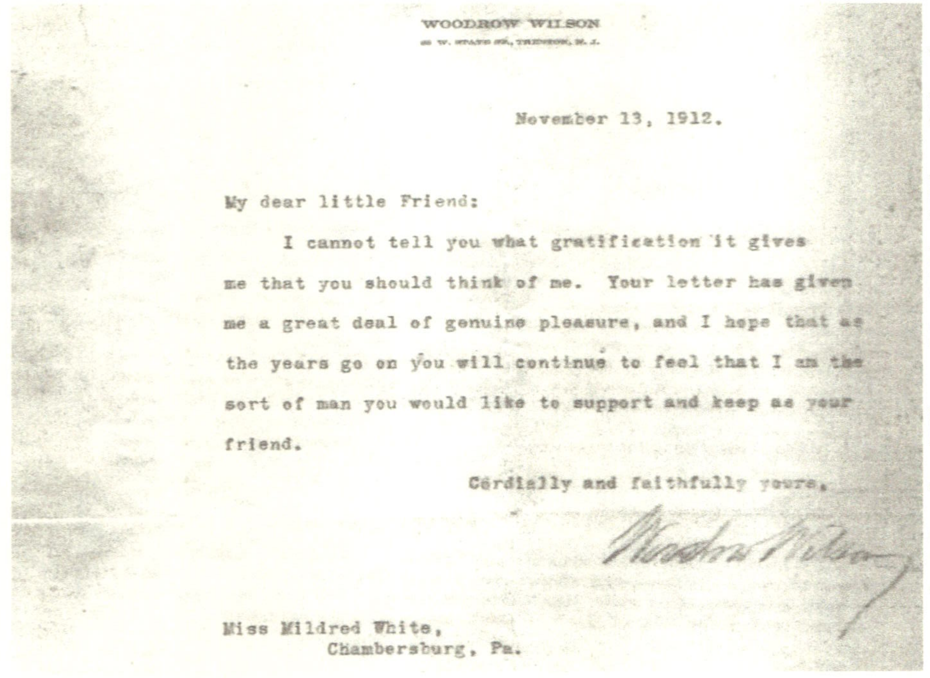

Letter from President Wilson to Miss Mildred White of Chambersburg, PA

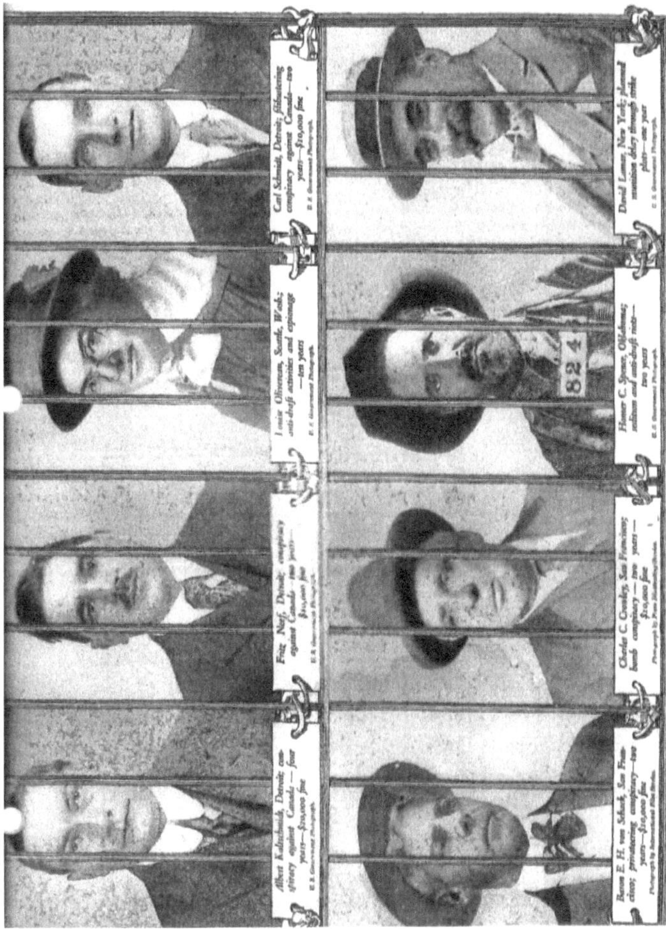

Many were accused of hindering the war effort, including David Lamar, who was accused of delaying munitions production by urging strikes.

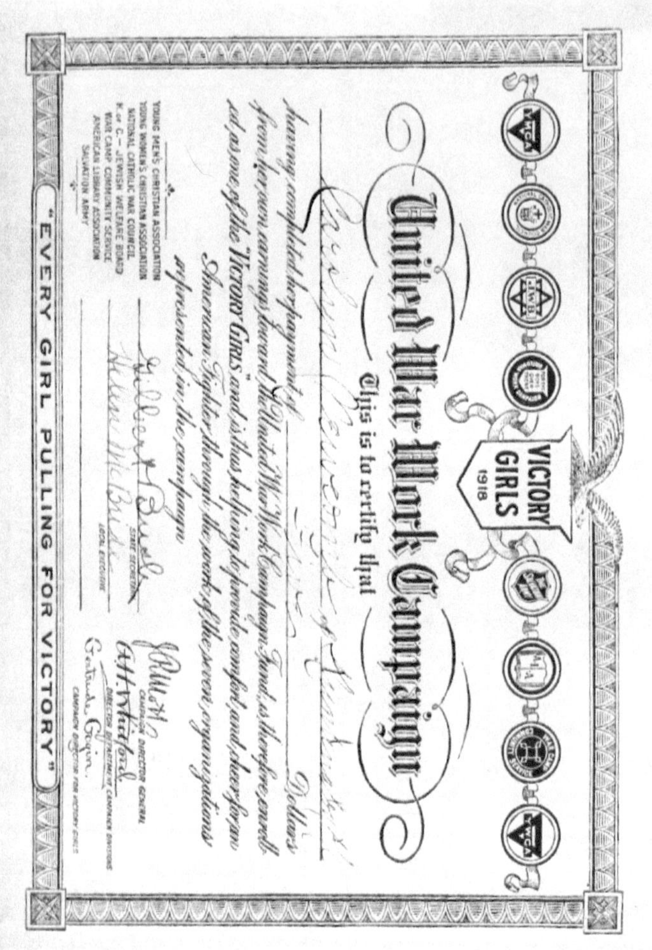

Victory Girls certificate from the United War Work Campaign

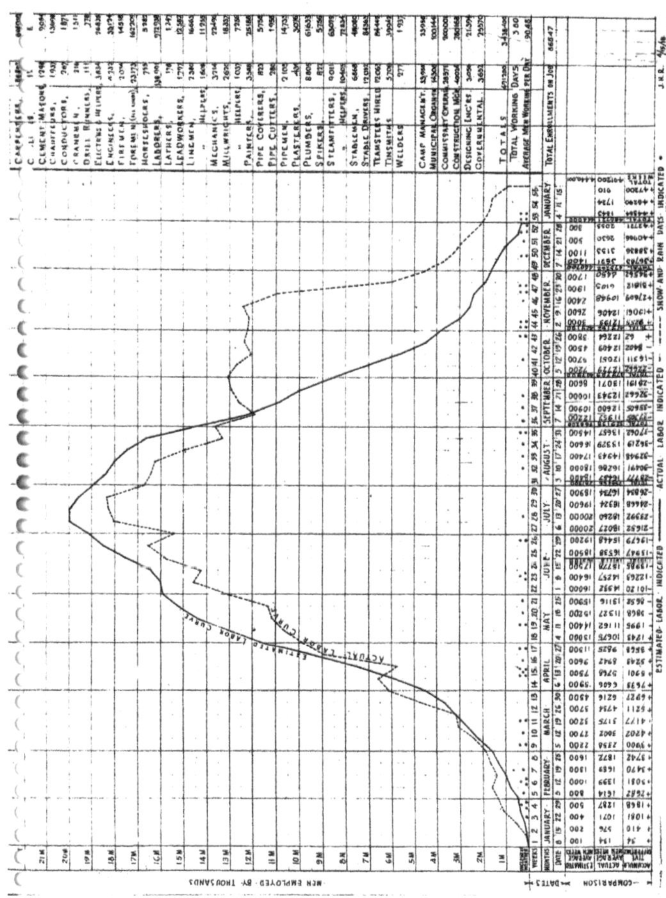

Labor chart

About the Author

Ann Moody Calwell spent her career as a teacher of English and Spanish, in addition to working as a play therapist for the children at West Virginia University Hospital and as a coordinator for the West Virginia Department of Education's Youth and Government Seminar programs. She lives in West Virginia with her husband, Stuart Calwell, with whom she shares daughters Elisa and Emily.

Ann Calwell

Ann's father, Jack C. Moody, served in the U.S. Army Corps in World War II. He worked as a chemical engineer at American Viscose Corporation's plant in Nitro during the town's second wave of manufacturing, two decades after the emergency production of gunpowder for World War I that Ana witnesses in the novel. Jack Moody also founded the Nitro World War I Memorial Museum. He was named a West Virginia History Hero in 1999.

*Ann Calwell's parents, Jack C. and Iva S.
Moody*